A Political Adventure Filled with Stories, Photos, Speeches, Cartoons, and Trivia

Democrat's Soul

A Tried-and-True View of Everything Blue

Health Communications, Inc.
Deerfield Beach, Florida

www.hcibooks.com

The views and opinions expressed in *Democrat's Soul* are those of the contributors and do not necessarily reflect the views and opinions of Health Communications, Inc., or its employees.

Library of Congress Cataloging-in-Publication Data is available from the Library of Congress.

© 2008 Health Communications Inc.
ISBN-10: 0-7573-0675-6
ISBN-13: 978-7573-0675-4

Publisher: Health Communications, Inc.
3201 S.W. 15th Street
Deerfield Beach, FL 33442-8190

All speeches reprinted in this book are from www.americanrhetoric.com.

Edited by Andrea Gold
Trivia, pages 34, 62, 118, 152, 176, by Dan Murphy
Cover photo © Fotolia.com
Cover design by Larissa Hise Henoch
Interior design and formatting by Lawna Patterson Oldfield
Photos pages 61 and 117 © Time & Life Pictures/Getty Images
Photo page 85 © Popperfoto/Getty Images
Photos pages 30, 151, and 203 © Getty Images
Photo page 175 © AFP/Getty Images

Contents

Introduction

Politics. The word alone evokes a vast array of emotions. In the context of our lives, politics conjures up imagery, memories, opinions, and heated debates, and the word "politics"—in and of itself—can't help but be extremely personal.

For many, making a party affiliation (no matter the party) can be one of the most defining and memorable moments of one's life. Your own political beliefs are a testament to your character, igniting your passions, strengthening your convictions, and exemplifying what you hold most dear and true in your heart. In *Democrat's Soul*, we set out on a journey to explore the personal significance that being a Democrat has on one's own history, development, ideologies, relationships, and so much more.

Democrat's Soul is not only an exploration, but a commemoration of the nostalgia and pride each party member has for its founders, its fighters, and its future. And what you'll find throughout these pages encapsulates good old Democrat zeal with compelling first-person stories from fellow Democrats, wit and wisdom from some of your favorite leaders, historical tidbits, and photos that illustrate the pivotal moments in Democrat history. Along the way, you'll laugh at clever cartoons, reminisce while reading excerpts from inspiring Democrat speeches, and test your political knowledge with trivia and must-know facts.

All in all, this political pick-me-up will entertain, educate, inspire, and give you a tried-and-true view of everything blue.

Democratic
Presidential Time Line

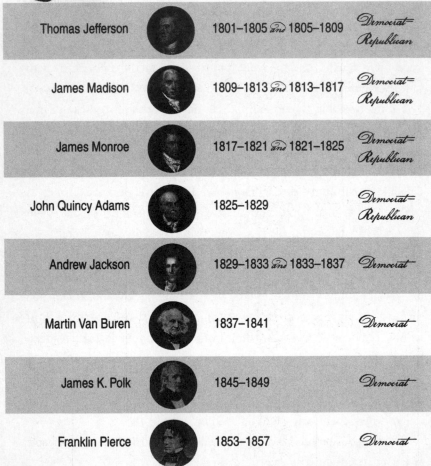

Thomas Jefferson		1801–1805 *and* 1805–1809	*Democrat-Republican*
James Madison		1809–1813 *and* 1813–1817	*Democrat-Republican*
James Monroe		1817–1821 *and* 1821–1825	*Democrat-Republican*
John Quincy Adams		1825–1829	*Democrat-Republican*
Andrew Jackson		1829–1833 *and* 1833–1837	*Democrat*
Martin Van Buren		1837–1841	*Democrat*
James K. Polk		1845–1849	*Democrat*
Franklin Pierce		1853–1857	*Democrat*

James Buchanan		1857–1861	*Democrat*
Andrew Johnson		1865–1869	*Democrat*
Grover Cleveland		1885–1889 *and* 1893–1897	*Democrat*
Woodrow Wilson		1913–1917 *and* 1917–1921	*Democrat*
Franklin D. Roosevelt		1933–1937 *and* 1937–1941 1941–1945 *and* 1945	*Democrat*
Harry S. Truman		1945–1949 *and* 1949–1953	*Democrat*
John F. Kennedy		1961–1963	*Democrat*
Lyndon B. Johnson		1963–1965 *and* 1965–1969	*Democrat*
James Earl Carter		1977–1981	*Democrat*
William J. Clinton		1993–1997 *and* 1997–2001	*Democrat*

He was honest.

He cared about the community.

He had good ideas.

Tony was my neighbor, and he was running for town council. It was 1975. I was in high school, Richard Nixon had just resigned, and the Vietnam War was coming to a close. America was changing, and my neighbor Tony was going to help make things better.

Tony was in his early thirties. He lived in the split-level ranch next door with his wife and their two small children. One of my sisters babysat for the kids. I raked their yard. Tony was excited about becoming a member of the town council. He was running against a longtime incumbent, and he wasn't supposed to have a chance. Everyone but Tony knew that he couldn't win.

I remember the night Tony announced his candidacy to my parents. We sat on my parents' back porch as Tony pleaded his case. "This town needs change," he told them. "We need to be represented." And he was right. We lived in a small, new development in rural northeastern Connecticut. The development and its residents were markedly different from the farms and Yankee farmers surrounding it. The needs of the commuting suburbanites were very different from those of the more entrenched farmers. The suburbanites required more services from the town, and the political landscape was changing.

"Do I have your vote?" Tony finally asked my mom and dad.

Without hesitation, my father answered him: "We don't vote."

Tony was flabbergasted. "Never?" he asked. "You've never voted?" They hadn't, and my dad made it clear that they weren't about to start now. Tony looked to my mother for help. She shook her head.

Over and over, Tony asked my parents why they didn't vote, and the answer was always the same: it didn't matter. They didn't believe their votes would make a difference.

Tony spent the next half-hour trying to convince my parents to register to vote. He talked about civic duty, about responsibility to the community, and about making the town better for their children. Tony talked until my parents were out of polite patience. Finally, Tony made a personal appeal.

"Will you do it for me? Will you do it just to help your neighbor?" They politely refused. Tony finally gave up.

Tony ran a great grassroots campaign. He walked door to door and talked to everyone who would listen. He was honest, he cared about the community, and he had good ideas. With each passing day, Tony closed the gap on the longtime incumbent.

In the final days before the election, Tony tried repeatedly to convince my parents to vote. I remember him telling them, "This is going to be a very close election. I'm going to need every vote." Mom and Dad were unmoved.

You've probably figured out the end of this story. After all, it is pretty predictable. Tony lost by a single vote. Had my parents voted for him, he would have won by a single vote. Things were never the same between Tony and my parents. I never saw them speak again. About six months after the election, Tony put his house up for sale. It sold quickly, and Tony and his family moved away less than a year after the election.

My parents never considered Tony's defeat their fault. They often discussed it, but only with each other. It always seemed to me that they just couldn't admit, even to themselves, that they were wrong about their votes not counting. My parents never did register to vote. My mother passed several years ago; she lived her whole life without ever casting a vote. Dad is nearly eighty, and also has no intention of ever voting.

The incident had a lasting effect on me. I registered to vote the day I was eligible, and I've voted in every election—major and minor—since then. Even when I was in the service and far from home, I voted in every election. My sisters mailed information to me about the issues and candidates, and I cast absentee ballots. I voted in several presidential elections this way. Both of my sisters were similarly affected. They, too, vote in every election.

And the best part is that my children have learned the lesson, too. All three of my daughters vote—in every election. We live in Florida, and we were here for the Florida 2000 election debacle. My entire family—except for my youngest daughter, who was too young to vote then—voted in that election. We watched the election night results together until the wee hours of the morning. Like many others, we were greeted that Wednesday morning, after very little sleep, with the news that the election had not been decided.

I was thrilled when my youngest daughter told me: "You're right, Dad. Every vote does count!" Even though she was too young to vote in that election, she learned the same lesson I had learned twenty-five years before: even if it is cliché, every vote does count, and we all have a responsibility to vote.

By their example, my parents taught me that every vote counts, and their refusal to vote actually determined the outcome of an election. I learned by watching my parents do the wrong thing. I wanted my daughters to learn by the right example, and so I took at least one of them to the polling place every time I voted. Not only did I create fond memories of holding one of my daughters' hands while casting my vote, I also feel I helped them understand the responsibility we all have as citizens. By sharing the story of Tony's heartbreaking run for office, I gave them a real-life example of the truth in the statement that "every vote counts."

C. A. Verno

Howdy Doody Democrat

My first political confrontation happened in 1960 when I was in third grade. I wore a John F. Kennedy campaign button to school, and a sixth-grader called me a liberal and tried to rip it off my Howdy Doody/Clarabell T-shirt. The button had a picture of JFK in the middle and the words "Students for Kennedy." I didn't know I was a liberal. I don't think I even knew I was a student. Well, the worm turned, and at seven years old, I could no longer afford to be apolitical.

Before this incident, most of my quarrels had to do with the great Yankee/Bosox wars that broke out every summer like poison ivy. If you lived in Connecticut, you were a New York Yankee fan, a Boston Red Sox fan, or a commie. The Yankee/Bosox wars tore apart more families than the Civil War and no-fault divorces combined—including mine. I lived and died with the Yankees, and my dad, a Sox fan, knew all he had to do to see me tear up with anger was declare, "Mickey Mantle's a bum" or "Roger Maris is a Republican."

I don't know why Roger Maris being a Republican upset me. I wasn't even sure what a Republican was, but I knew I hated them worse than the times tables. The 1960 presidential campaign made me and most other third-graders in Plantsville's South End Elementary School put aside previously significant things like baseball and penmanship. This was playground politics at its most repugnant. Every recess, insults were hurled ("Nanny-nanny-nanny goat, Kennedy's a billy goat"), Mighty Mouse lunch boxes were stomped, and Twinkies were lobbed. Personally, I never wasted a Twinkie—an apple, maybe; a carrot, certainly—but not a Twinkie. My youthful brain couldn't understand why anyone would choose Nixon over Kennedy. Nixon was from California—the weirdo state—while Kennedy was one of us—a New Englander. Kennedy was a Democrat, while Nixon was a stinkin' Republican. Why, just saying the word "Republican" would make my mouth scrunch up like I had a mouthful of turnips.

If Richard Nixon played baseball, I thought, he'd play for the Red Sox—then I'd spit. I always spit after I said "Red Sox," so I had to be careful not to utter those words at the dinner table or in church. I made no secret of the reason I backed Kennedy. It wasn't his foreign policy, his economic strategy, or his dodge ball abilities. It was because I had a wicked crush on his wife, Jackie. My father and I may have disagreed about baseball, but we agreed on Jackie—hubba, hubba. I also supported Kennedy because he was Catholic, as was I.

Actually, until that election, I thought everybody was Catholic. I'd heard of Jewish people, but I thought they were Jewish Catholics. One night Walter Cronkite reported that Kennedy might lose votes because he was Catholic. It was then that my mother explained to me that not everyone was Catholic—in fact, *she* wasn't Catholic. First, no Easter Bunny, then no Tooth Fairy, and now my mother wasn't Catholic! What next, no Santa? That wasn't the worst of it. Not only was Mom not Catholic—she was Mormon! I didn't know a Mormon from a Republican, but I'd seen pictures of them in covered wagons, and they all had beards—even the women.

After a stiff drink of Ovaltine, I managed to put the Mormon thing on the back burner and ask why some people wouldn't vote for a

Catholic. Mom told me that people were afraid that if a Catholic were elected, the Pope would run the country. I wasn't sure I wanted the Pope running the country either, and this information almost put me in the Nixon camp. I mean, I was a Catholic, sure, but not to a fault. I figured if the Pope ran the country, he might make us learn Latin, and I was having a hard enough time passing third-grade English. The following year I'd be ready to give up Catholicism completely after discovering that only Catholics couldn't eat meat on Friday. I hated fish, and vegetarians weren't invented yet. I tried to talk my parents into letting me join the Methodists, at least on Fridays.

My mother, "The Mormon," as I now regarded her, might've gone for it, but my Irish Catholic father would have none of it. I outsmarted them, though—I gave up fish for Lent every year. So, thanks to Catholicism, baseball, and Jacqueline Bouvier Kennedy, the die was cast: I was a lifelong Democrat. I've only voted for a Republican presidential candidate once. That was in 1972 when I voted for . . . you guessed it, Richard Nixon. I also now live in California—the weirdo state—and I hate the Yankees more than the times tables. I even enjoy a nice swordfish steak now and again. Life has a way of doing that—throwing you an occasional curveball.

James Alexander

In Search of the Truth, I Found My Party

Growing up in the 1970s in a family split by divorce, I had my first exposure to politics at the age of ten by a babysitter who would talk to me and my sister and brother about the upcoming 1976 presidential election between Gerald Ford and Jimmy Carter. She liked Ford, so we did, too. We would find photos of Jimmy Carter in the newspaper and draw mustaches and devil's horns on his image. We took his successful election with disappointment, like our team losing the World Series. As a result of this early experience, I became engrossed as a fourteen-year-old in the 1980 presidential election. I remember the feelings of powerlessness that the nation was experiencing during the Iranian hostage crisis as I watched ABC's *America Held Hostage* with Ted Koppel every night. President Jimmy Carter seemed to be the symbol of that powerlessness, or at least that was the impression that the media would have us believe. Being a young teen at the time, I earnestly believed what the Republicans were saying: President Carter's weakness and incompetence in bringing home the hostages meant he lacked the characteristics of a good leader. Ronald Reagan was the man for the job, as he would restore honor, courage, and character to the office of president. I remembered looking up to Reagan as a father figure. My own father lived separately from my mother, sister, brother, and me, and he was a liberal Democrat to boot. I was mesmerized by Reagan's image: a strong, tough-minded older man who would stand up for our demoralized nation.

Four years later, I cast my first vote at the age of eighteen for Ronald Reagan in the 1984 presidential election. By this time I was known as the Alex P. Keaton of my family, the only Republican in a family of Democrats. I would continue to be a Republican for the next ten years, voting for George H.W. Bush in 1988 and 1992. It seemed that I would be a life-long Republican. But then something happened.

My first job out of college was teaching high-school English in the New York Public Schools, and I needed to complete a relevant graduate degree in order to maintain my state certification to teach. I had previously taken education courses and wanted to try a different direction in my graduate studies. My local college offered an interdisciplinary graduate program in which one could select courses from different departments. The first course that I took was a combined History of Western Culture and History of Philosophy course. I had never taken Philosophy 101 as an undergraduate, and I had heard that philosophy was a difficult area of study. Sitting in the first seminar, I was immediately turned on. My professor handed out a sheet with a list of the "big questions" and discussed the significance of each. I was hooked. We studied the pre-Socratic philosophers, Plato, Aristotle, the Stoics, the Epicureans, St. Augustine, and Thomas Aquinas. I was particularly interested in Plato's and Aristotle's ideas about politics. During that first semester in graduate school, I became a serious student and a truth-seeker. Later, I took another course in which I was further enlightened about politics and power.

One day, the professor of my politics and media class explained two theories of American democracy: the first one was the populist model that stated that the people have the power in society, and generate the laws and policies of the nation through their representatives who have their best interests in mind; the second theory was the elite model, which said that there is a plutocratic elite that ultimately has reigning influence over legislators and presidents in the pursuit of their own narrow interests. This elite is identified with the owners and directors of large corporations, and they use their corporate control of the media to shape the public's perceived reality in order to benefit their accumulation of wealth and power. I had never heard of the elite theory, but when my professor asked the class which theory we believed was more accurate, most people, including myself, agreed on the elite model. That set me off into investigating the truth of the theory.

As part of our class requirements, our professor had us subscribe to *The Nation* magazine and the *New York Times*. I still subscribe to both of these publications. I read several books on the subject, including *The Power Elite*, *The Media Monopoly*, and *When Corporations Rule the World*, and I came away with the belief that the "little guy" like you and me is manipulated, propagandized, and ignored by those who have the real power in society. My independent study of these books led me to the writings of Noam Chomsky and Howard Zinn. Before I knew what had happened to me, I realized I was no longer a Republican.

I now know that the whole Reagan "revolution" was a highly manipulative illusion concocted by cynical political operators ultimately influenced by the power elite. They presented their "leading man" as a strong, tough father figure to lead our nation out of despair. The problem with this "cure" to the malaise of the Carter Administration was that the same group of people who brought it on was the one offering the solution. Eisenhower, perhaps one Republican who is deserving of respect, called it correctly in his farewell address when he warned of "undue influence of the military-industrial complex," which is synonymous with the power elite who brought us the Vietnam War. That war and its excess spending, many historians believe, was partly responsible for the tough economic times in the late seventies when "stagflation" was rampant. The Iranian hostage crisis was an example of "the chickens coming home to roost" as the power elite in the 1950s had the Shah installed in a coup of the elected Iranian democracy. By controlling the media, the power elite managed to make the crisis seem like Jimmy Carter's fault, thus paving the way for Reagan.

Looking back on my political affiliations, I have been deeply disappointed by the truth of Ronald Reagan's presidency. As a young person, I feel that I was manipulated by the Reagan spectacle. It's despicable that such manipulation of the populace can go on in our nation. Yet it does today. Looking around me, the only hope Americans have to look out for their best interests and fight against the influence of the power elite is the Democratic Party. Republican leaders and apologists unabashedly support the interests of the power elite. Conversely, Democrats have a long history of being the "people's party." From Andrew Jackson to William Jennings Bryan to Franklin Delano Roosevelt to even Lyndon Johnson, Democrats have, for the most part, sought to make sure the average American's interests were a priority. Of course, they have to engage in a political environment in which the power elite usually gets its way, so compromise is often necessary in order to accomplish some of the people's interests.

The Democratic Party is not perfect. Some members firmly support the interests of the power elite over the interests of the people, but I believe that the progressive wing of the party is the best hope for the future of the party and the American people. The more the Democratic Party aligns itself with economically conservative views, the more it serves the interest of the power elite. I have hope that Democrats will embrace their progressive history and serve the interests of the people. More than ever, Americans need the Democratic Party to be the Democratic Party.

Today, I see Jimmy Carter as the better president (than Reagan). Working in a compromised system, he did his best to pursue policies that benefited average Americans. I believe he handled the Iranian hostage situation with poise, nuance, and wisdom. If he had sent the troops in for a full-scale invasion, the hostages would have been killed, and our nation would have been involved in a Middle East war. He successfully saw the crisis to the end with the safe return of the hostages without war. I wonder how George W. Bush would have handled that situation. Today, Jimmy Carter is one of our greatest statesmen, tirelessly working for peace in the Middle East and the eradication of disease in third world countries. I'm proud that he was our president.

I find that I have come full circle in my life and politics. When I was young, my teenage rebellion took the form of embracing the conservatism of Reagan as opposed to my father's liberalism of Mario Cuomo. During my twenties I went on a quest for truth, leading me wherever it would. I found the truth of politics and power in our nation, and it transformed me. I've since come back from my journey and settled into a life of public service, as a teacher and union leader, and most significantly as a liberal, progressive Democrat. Today, my father and I share almost identical views on politics and the need to elect a Democratic President and Congress. I hope the people wake up and take back our government from the control of the power elite.

Matthew J. Rottino

Flashy Campaigning

My mom walked up to the door and knocked, her hands full of literature for my dad's campaign. To her surprise, a man answered the door in nothing but a towel.

"Good evening, sir. My husband, Elbert Gill, is running for re-election and would really appreciate your vote." The man dropped his towel and stood there with nothing on but his birthday suit.

My dad was the state representative for our district for twenty years. He was a self-titled "Ol' Southern Democrat," which meant that he was conservative, but fought for the blue-collar workers and the little guys who couldn't help themselves.

This gritty work ethic ran through his veins and was reflected in the way he conducted his campaigns. Every two years, our backyard was full of screen-printing equipment, drying signs, and wooden stakes— all to help spread the campaign word around the neighborhood. My dad was old-fashioned. There were no TV commercials or expensive mailings; everything was hands-on and face-to-face. The goal was simple: meet as many people in the district as possible. Several nights a week, we went with friends and knocked on each and every door, no matter the neighborhood. He did this not only to make personal contact with the community, but to unleash his secret weapon—my mom.

Campaigning door to door was her forte. My dad used to say that she could "sweet-talk a vote out of the toughest opposition." It was natural for her to go up to the door, introduce herself, talk about Dad, ask for a vote, and request permission to place a sign in the yard. Maybe it was her smile or just the southern charm that comes from growing up on a cotton farm. Whatever the case, she almost always elicited a positive response. The vast majority of her encounters were with good people, people often called "the salt of the earth." Sometimes she crossed paths with an angry dog and was forced to jump fences. Even rarer was the angry objector—a person who disliked my father and his leadership. However, in more than twenty years of politics, my mom never encountered a flasher—until that day. When most people would have stuttered, stammered, or stared, she just kept talking. "Would you mind if we put a sign in your yard? Thank you, and I hope we have your support!"

I have no idea of the guy's response. All I know is that my mom never missed a beat, never got flustered in the heat of the embarrassing moment. Who knows the guy's motive? Maybe he just thought it would be funny to shock a woman twice his age, or maybe he was just a sick pervert.

What I do know is my mom acted as if it was the most normal occurrence to be flashed by a prospective voter. She returned to the group to share this crazy campaign story. My dad hit the roof and wanted to have words with the guy, but mom said no. It would really look bad to have the state representative take the law into his own hands. "He wasn't much to look at, Elbert," she said. "And besides, he was probably voting Republican."

Scott Gill

Blue Sheep of the Family

I was born into a staunch Republican family that enjoyed Sunday dinners at Grandma and Grandpa's house, complete with KFC and Dunkin' Donuts for dessert. My family didn't argue politics outright, but rather made their fierce stance well-known through protestations about "those damn _____" (insert the inappropriate racial tag of your choice here), while smiling down at me, their little bundle of joy, and chiding me sweetly to stay away from such types—they only brought bad news.

My family figured they paid a lot of taxes to maintain the distance between "us" and "them" and always voted Republican. They also figured the old white guys understood their concerns far better than those young men from the East Coast, and the ballots they turned in required little effort as they always voted a straight Republican ticket.

I spent the better part of my growing-up years in a world of white faces attending Catholic school and church on Sunday mornings before heading back to Grandma and Grandpa's for more fried chicken and minority-bashing. I had little knowledge about the other racial groups; they only existed in the images I saw on the console TV. I just knew that we were better than they were, and we had all the answers.

This was my happy existence—not meeting anyone who wasn't white or middle-class—until I started high school at the age of fourteen, the same year the first black mayoral candidate in Chicago came to our church to speak to the congregation. Before he was due to arrive that fateful Sunday morning, members of our congregation spray-painted "Go home, n–––r" on the side of our church. I remember staring at the words and being repulsed by the hatred and sickened by the knowledge that the people I sat in church with every week could write such a horrible thing. That was my turning point. I began to see the world through much different eyes.

After graduating from college, I taught at schools located in the worst neighborhoods of Chicago and Detroit. I started my own college-preparatory charter school on the all-black west side of Chicago, enduring repeated protests by my mother to get a "respectable" job in the suburbs. I helped set up similar schools for disadvantaged youth in inner cities across America.

My Republican family stayed in front of their televisions, continuing their tirades, albeit a bit more discreetly. Uncles would go into a rage when I would talk about doing more to help people on welfare, raising the minimum wage, or supporting Head Start. They would wonder where they had gone wrong with me. I voted Democrat, supported the Democrats, and was desperate for a way to do more.

On March 18, 2003, George W. Bush ordered the invasion of Iraq. I was vehemently opposed to the idea of the war, understanding that the majority of victims would be innocent civilians who had nothing to do with al-Qaeda or 9/11. I was sick about the whole thing. I knew I could protest to my heart's content, but that the Republicans at the White House would simply do what they wanted. Then I realized that their actions were funded by federal tax dollars. By paying federal taxes, I was contributing to the funding of the arms, ammunition, and supplies utilized in Iraq. Simply refusing to pay my taxes would only land me in jail, and would result in fines and late fees—funding the war machine even more. I came up with the only solution my mind could wrap itself around: I would leave the country and not return until a Democrat was in the White House *or* until the war ended, whichever came first.

My plan was to work as an aid worker, helping others while also promoting a more positive image of Americans in the world. While I was helping those in need in other countries, I could also legally avoid paying federal taxes to the Republican machine that ran Washington. I was a liberal Democrat on a mission, and in June 2003, I quit my job, stored all my possessions, and sold my car. My Republican family saw me off as the big Lufthansa plane ("She can't even fly on American planes!") took off for Africa, all the while shaking their heads and chuckling to each other that I would be back when I realized there weren't any flush toilets in the desert.

Five years later, I am still overseas. Since 2003, I have worked and lived in four countries and am preparing to move to my fifth. I plan to return to the United States in January 2009, if Mr. Obama or Mrs. Clinton makes it possible for me to do so. Sure, I occasionally visit America, but I am careful to stay no longer than the thirty-five days that I am allowed annually in order to retain my federal tax-exempt status. I have since acquired a husband from the Netherlands (my family no doubt thinking, "Bunch of drug-using, gay marriage-loving liberals . . ."), and a very open-minded two-year-old son who holds four citizenships. The best part? I have not paid a penny in federal income taxes in five years.

My greatest moment as a Democrat occurred in May 2005 when George Bush came to The Hague to take part in a ceremony honoring veterans that served in World War II. Through some bizarre happenstance, I was invited to have breakfast with Mr. Bush and twenty-four other "lucky" Americans living in the Netherlands. My family in America was so excited for me at this rare opportunity. But I just couldn't imagine myself at the table with this man and all that he represented. I knew that I would honor my principles and not attend. I sent back the invitation with the RSVP: "Sorry, I wouldn't be able to afford bail." My family still hasn't forgotten that, and for very different reasons, and with great pride, neither have I.

Nancy Ellen Claxton

Reprinted by permission of Mark Parisi. ©2008 Mark Parisi.

WHO SAID IT?

It is to be regretted that the rich and powerful too often bend the acts of government to their own selfish purposes.

—*Andrew Jackson*

It is the responsibility of the citizens to support their government. It is not the responsibility of the government to support its citizens.

—*Grover Cleveland*

You cannot stop the spread of an idea by passing a law against it.

—*Harry S. Truman*

We need a spirit of community, a sense that we are all in this together. If we have no sense of community, the American dream will wither.

—*William Clinton*

A good leader
can't get too far ahead
of his followers.
—*Franklin Delano Roosevelt*

The American,
by nature, is optimistic.
He is experimental, an
inventor, and a builder who
builds best when called
upon to build greatly.
—*John F. Kennedy*

An honest man
can feel no pleasure in the
exercise of power over his
fellow citizens.
—*Thomas Jefferson*

For this is what America is all about.
It is the uncrossed desert and the
unclimbed ridge. It is the star that is not
reached and the harvest sleeping in
the unplowed ground. . . .
—*Lyndon B. Johnson*

William Jennings Bryan

Democratic National Convention Address

"A Cross of Gold"

Delivered July 8, 1896

M r. Chairman and Gentlemen of the Convention: I would be presumptuous, indeed, to present myself against the distinguished gentlemen to whom you have listened if this were mere measuring of abilities; but this is not a contest between persons. The humblest citizen in all the land, when clad in the armor of a righteous cause, is stronger than all the hosts of error. I come to speak to you in defense of a cause as holy as the cause of liberty—the cause of humanity.

When this debate is concluded, a motion will be made to lay upon the table the resolution offered in commendation of the Administration, and also the resolution offered in condemnation of the Administration. We object to bringing this question down to the level of persons. The individual is but an atom; he is born, he acts, he dies; but principles are eternal, and this has been a contest over a principle.

Never before in the history of this country has there been witnessed such a contest as that through which we have just passed. Never before in the history of American politics has a great issue been fought out as this issue has been, by the voters of a great party. On the fourth of March, 1895, a few Democrats, most of them members of Congress, issued an address to the Democrats of the nation, asserting that the money question was the paramount issue of the hour; declaring that a majority of the Democratic party had the right to control the action of the party on this paramount issue; and concluding with the request that the believers in the free coinage of silver in the Democratic party should organize, take charge of and control the policy of the Democratic party.

Three months later, at Memphis, an organization was perfected, and the silver Democrats went forth openly and courageously proclaiming their belief, and declaring that, if successful, they would crystallize into a platform the declaration which they had made. Then began the conflict. With a zeal approaching the zeal which inspired the crusaders who followed Peter the Hermit, our silver Democrats went forth from victory unto victory, until they are now assembled, not to discuss, not to debate, but to enter up the judgment already rendered by the plain people of this country. In this contest, brother has been arrayed against brother, father against son. The warmest ties of love, acquaintance and association have been disregarded; old leaders have been cast aside when they have refused to give expression to the sentiments of those whom they would lead, and new leaders have sprung up to give direction to this cause of truth. Thus has the contest been waged, and we have assembled here under as binding and solemn instructions as were ever imposed upon representatives of the people.

We do not come as individuals. As individuals we might have been glad to compliment the gentleman from New York [Senator Hill], but we know that the people for whom we speak would never be willing to put him in a position where he could thwart the will of the

Democratic party. I say it was not a question of persons; it was a question of principle, and it is not with gladness, my friends, that we find ourselves brought into conflict with those who are now arrayed on the other side.

The gentleman who preceded me [ex-Governor Russell] spoke of the State of Massachusetts; let me assure him that not one present in all this convention entertains the least hostility to the people of the State of Massachusetts, but we stand here representing people who are the equals before the law, of the greatest citizens in the State of Massachusetts. When you [turning to the gold delegates] come before us and tell us that we are about to disturb your business interests, we reply that you have disturbed our business interests by your course.

We say to you that you have made the definition of a business man too limited in its application. The man who is employed for wages is as much a business man as his employer; the attorney in a country town is as much a business man as the corporation counsel in a great metropolis; the merchant at the cross-roads store is as much a business man as the merchant of New York; the farmer who goes forth in the morning and toils all day—who begins in the spring and toils all summer—and who by the application of brain and muscle to the natural resources of the country creates wealth, is as much a business man as the man who goes upon the board of trade and bets upon the price of grain; the miners who go down a thousand feet into the earth, or climb two thousand feet upon the cliffs, and bring forth from their hiding places the precious metals to be poured into the channels of trade are as much business men as the few financial magnates who, in a back room, corner the money of the world. We come to speak for this broader class of business men.

Ah, my friends, we say not one word against those who live upon the Atlantic coast, but the hardy pioneers who have braved all the dangers of the wilderness, who have made the desert to blossom as the rose—the pioneers away out there [pointing to the West], who rear their children near to Nature's heart, where they can mingle their voices with the voices of the birds—out there where they have erected schoolhouses for the education of their young, churches where they praise their Creator, and cemeteries where rest the ashes of their dead—these people, we say, are as deserving of the consideration of our party as any people in this country. It is for these that we speak. We do not come as aggressors. Our war is not a war of conquest; we are fighting in the defense of our homes, our families, and posterity. We have petitioned, and our petitions have been scorned; we have entreated, and our entreaties have been disregarded; we have begged, and they have mocked when our calamity came. We beg no longer; we entreat no more; we petition no more. We defy them.

The gentleman from Wisconsin has said that he fears a Robespierre. My friends, in this land of the free you need not fear that a tyrant will spring up from among the people. What we need is an Andrew Jackson to stand, as Jackson stood, against the encroachments of organized wealth. They tell us that this platform was made to catch votes. We reply to them that changing conditions make new issues; that the principles upon which Democracy rests are as everlasting as the hills, but that they must be applied to new conditions as they arise. Conditions have arisen, and we are here to meet these conditions. They tell us that the income tax ought not to be brought in here; that it is a new idea. They criticize us for our criticism of the Supreme Court of the United States. My friends, we have not criticized; we have simply called attention to what you already know. If you want criticisms, read the dissenting opinions of the court. There you will find criticism. They say that we passed an unconstitutional law; we deny it. The income tax law was not unconstitutional when it was passed; it was not unconstitutional when it went before the Supreme Court for the first time; it did not become unconstitutional until one of the judges changed his mind, and we cannot be expected to know when a judge will change his mind. The income tax is just. It simply intends to put the burdens of government justly upon the backs of the people. I am in favor of an income tax. When I find a man who is not willing to bear his share of the burdens of the government which protects him, I find a man who is unworthy to enjoy the blessings of a government like ours.

They say that we are opposing national bank currency. It is true. If you will read what Thomas Benton said you will find he said that, in searching history, he would find but one parallel to Andrew Jackson; that was Cicero, who destroyed the conspiracy of Cataline and saved Rome. Benton said that Cicero only did for Rome what Jackson did for us when he destroyed the bank conspiracy and saved America. We say in our platform that we believe that the right to coin and issue money is a function of government. We believe it. We believe that it is a part of sovereignty, and can no more with safety be delegated to private individuals than we could afford to delegate to private individuals the power to make penal statutes or levy taxes. Mr. Jefferson, who was once regarded as good Democratic authority, seems to have differed in opinion from the gentleman who has addressed us on the part of the minority. Those who are opposed to this proposition tell us that the issue of paper money is a function of the bank, and that the Government ought to go out of the banking business. I stand with Jefferson rather than with them, and tell them, as he did, that the issue of money is a function of government, and that the banks ought to go out of the governing business.

They complain about the plank which declares against life tenure in office. They have tried to strain it to mean that which it does not mean. What we oppose by that plank is the life tenure which is being built up in Washington, and which excludes from participation in official benefits the humbler members of society. Let me call your attention to two or three important things. The gentleman from New York says that he will propose an amendment to the platform providing that the proposed change in our monetary system shall not affect contracts already made. Let me remind you that there is no intention of affecting those contracts which according to present laws are made payable in gold. But if he means to say that we cannot change our monetary system without protecting those who have loaned money before the change was made, I desire to ask him where, in law or in morals, he can find justification for not protecting the debtors when the act of 1873 was passed, if he now insists that we must protect the creditors.

He says he will also propose an amendment which will provide for the suspension of free coinage if we fail to maintain the parity within a year. We reply that when we advocate a policy which we believe will be successful, we are not compelled to raise a doubt as to our own sincerity by suggesting what we shall do if we fail. I ask him, if he would apply his logic to us, why he does not apply it to himself. He says he wants this country to try to secure an international agreement. Why does he not tell us what he is going to do if he fails to secure an international agreement? There is more reason for him to do that than there is for us to provide against the failure to maintain the parity.

Our opponents have tried for twenty years to secure an international agreement, and those are waiting for it most patiently who do not want it at all.

And now, my friends, let me come to the paramount issue. If they ask us why it is that we say more on the money question than we say upon the tariff question, I reply that, if protection has slain its thousands, the gold standard has slain its tens of thousands. If they ask us why we do not embody in our platform all the things that we believe in, we reply that when we have restored the money of the Constitution, all other necessary reform will be possible, but that until this is done there is no other reform that can be accomplished.

Why is it that within three months such a change has come over the country? Three months ago, when it was confidently asserted that those who believe in the gold standard would frame our platform and nominate our candidates, even the advocates to the gold standard did not think that we could elect a President. And they had good reason for their doubt, because there is scarcely a State here to-day asking for the gold standard which is not in the absolute control of the Republican party. But note the change. Mr. McKinley was nominated at St. Louis upon a platform which declared for the maintenance of the gold standard until it can be changed into bimetallism by international agreement. Mr. McKinley was the most popular man among the Republicans, and three months ago everybody in the Republican party prophesied his election. How is it to-day? Why, the man who was once pleased to think that he looked like Napoleon—that man shudders to-day when he remembers that he was nominated on the anniversary of the battle of Waterloo. Not only that, but as he listens he can hear with ever-increasing distinctness the sound of the waves as they beat upon the lonely shores of St. Helena.

Why this change? Ah, my friends, is not the reason for the change evident to any one who will look at the matter? No private character, however pure, no personal popularity, however great, can protect from the avenging wrath of an indignant people a man who will declare that he is in favor of fastening the gold standard upon this country, or who is willing to surrender the right of self-government and place the legislative control of our affairs in the hands of foreign potentates and powers.

We go forth confident that we shall win. Why? Because upon the paramount issue of this campaign there is not a spot of ground upon which the enemy will dare to challenge battle. If they tell us that the gold standard is a good thing, we shall point to their platform and tell them that their platform pledges the party to get rid of the gold standard and substitute bimetallism. If the gold standard is a good thing, why try to get rid of it? I call your attention to the fact that some of the very people who are in this convention to-day, and who tell us that we ought to declare in favor of international bimetallism—thereby declaring that the gold standard is wrong and that the principle of bimetallism is better—these very people four months ago were open and avowed advocates of the gold standard, and were then telling us that we could not legislate two metals together, even with the aid of all the world. If the gold standard is a good thing, we ought to declare in favor of its retention, and not in favor of abandoning it, and if the gold standard is a bad thing, why should we wait until other nations are willing to help us to let go? Here is the line of battle, and we care not upon which issue they force the fight; we are prepared to meet them on either issue or on both. If they tell us that the gold standard is the standard of civilization, we reply to them that this, the most enlightened of all the nations of the earth, has never declared for a gold standard and that both the great parties this year are declaring against it. If the gold standard is the standard of civilization, why, my friends, should we not have it? If they come to meet us on that issue, we can present the history of our nation. More than that—we can tell them that they will search the pages of history in vain to find a single instance where the common people of any land have ever declared themselves in favor of the gold standard. They can find where the holders of fixed investments have declared for a gold standard, but not where the masses have.

Mr. Carlisle said in 1878 that this was a struggle between "the idle holders of idle capital" and "the struggling masses, who produce the wealth and pay the taxes of the country," and, my friends, the question we are to decide is, upon which side will the Democratic party fight—upon the side of "the idle holders of idle capital," or upon the side of "the struggling masses"? That is the question which the party must answer first, and then it must be answered by each individual hereafter. The sympathies of the Democratic party, as shown by the platform, are on the side of the struggling masses who have ever been the foundation of the Democratic party. There are two ideas of government. There are those who believe that if you will only legislate to make the well-to-do prosperous, their prosperity will leak through on those below. The Democratic idea, however, has been that if you legislate to make the masses prosperous, their prosperity will find its way up through every class which rests upon them.

You come to us and tell us that the great cities are in favor of the gold standard; we reply that the great cities rest upon our broad and fertile prairies. Burn down your cities and leave our farms, and your cities will spring up again as if by magic; but destroy our farms, and the grass will grow in the streets of every city in the country.

My friends, we declare that this nation is able to legislate for its own people on every question without waiting for the aid or consent of any other nation on earth, and upon that issue we expect to carry every State in the Union. I shall not slander the inhabitants of the fair State of Massachusetts nor the inhabitants of the State of New York by saying that, when they are confronted with the proposition, they will declare that this nation is not able to attend to its own business. It is the issue of 1776 over again. Our ancestors, when but

3,000,000 in number, had the courage to declare their political independence on every other nation; shall we, their descendants, when we have grown to 70,000,000, declare that we are less independent than our forefathers?

No, my friends, that will never be the verdict of our people. Therefore, we care not upon what lines the battle is fought. If they say bimetallism is good, but that we cannot have it until other nations help us, we reply that, instead of having a gold standard because England has, we will restore bimetallism, and then let England have bimetallism because the United States has it. If they dare to come out in the open field and defend the gold standard as a good thing, we will fight them to the uttermost. Having behind us the producing masses of this nation and the world, supported by the commercial interests, the laboring interests, and the toilers everywhere, we will answer their demand for a gold standard by saying to them: you shall not press down upon the brow of labor this crown of thorns; you shall not crucify mankind upon a cross of gold.

A great moment in Democratic history: American president Thomas Woodrow Wilson defends the Treaty of Versailles at the Paris Peace Conference around 1919. The Treaty signaled the end of World War I and was signed between Germany and the Allied Forces and the League of Nations was established.

Trivia

1. Who was the last Democrat from a northern state elected president?

2. Who is the only Democrat on Mount Rushmore?

3. What Democratic presidential candidate lost by the closest margin in the Electoral College?

4. When did the Democratic Party hold its first convention to nominate a candidate for president?

5. Who was the first Catholic to run for the presidency as the candidate of a major party?

6. When did Democrats start calling themselves "Democrats"?

7. Who was the first woman to have a place on the national ticket of a major party?

8. Who was the only man elected to nonconsecutive terms as president?

9. Who was the only man to serve as a senator from three states?

10. Who was the longest serving Speaker of the House?

1. John F. Kennedy in 1960

2. Thomas Jefferson

3. Samuel Tilden in the contested election of 1876. Tilden ended up losing to Rutherford B. Hayes by a vote of 185–184.

4. 1828, nominating Andrew Jackson for president

5. Alfred E. Smith in 1928

6. During Andrew Jackson's campaign for the presidency in 1828

7. Geraldine Ferraro, Walter Mondale's running mate in 1984

8. Grover Cleveland, the 22nd (1885–1889) and 24th (1893–1897) president

9. James Shields, who was elected senator from Illinois in 1848 and served one term, was elected senator from Minnesota in 1858 and served a year, and while living in Missouri was appointed to fill an unexpired term in 1879

10. Sam Rayburn of Texas. A representative from 1914 until his death in 1961, he was Speaker from 1940, except for the two congressional terms when the Republicans won the House in 1946 and 1952.

Tales of a Mixed Marriage

It was 1957. I was nineteen years old and living in Brooklyn, New York. I had fallen in love with a tall, handsome, twenty-four-year-old engineer from Queens. Ed and I had been dating for close to a year, and although we were ready for a permanent commitment, we knew we would have to wait. Conscription—mandatory military service—was still in effect that year, and Ed was due to be drafted.

Two months after we met, Ed and I realized we were different religions. After much discussion, we agreed we could overcome this obstacle with respect and understanding.

One night, Ed arrived to pick me up for our date wearing his I LIKE IKE button. I watched my mother's knees buckle, but she quickly regained her balance. My father just sighed and rolled his eyes. The rest of the family looked as if they had been turned to stone, but, thankfully, no one screamed or fainted. I was so proud of my blue-collar, staunchly Democratic family that night. I decided to tackle this new problem later, went out on our date, and had a great time.

The next morning, my family gathered around to offer their condolences and ask me what I was going to do. I assured them that I knew love could conquer all and that I still intended to accept Ed's proposal, if it came. At an opportune moment, I told Ed about my family's political affiliations. He just laughed and promised not to wear his I LIKE IKE button the next time he picked me up. We agreed that fate seemed to be conspiring against us, but we felt love and a great sense of humor were all we needed.

Ed was drafted that year, much to my parents' relief. They really liked Ed, but they felt that with him out of the picture, I might find a nice Catholic Democrat to marry.

Both our families had concerns about our marrying, but Ed and I knew we had something worth fighting for. We decided not to let their doubts jeopardize our relationship. So, despite the reelection of Dwight D. Eisenhower, we became engaged after Ed's tour of duty. In September 1959, this Irish-Catholic Democrat married her wonderful German-Protestant Republican.

Ed and I lived in a two-family house with his mother and his older brother and his family while we were looking for a house. Ed's family were and still are dedicated Republicans. I knew they hadn't been too happy about my religion, but I never asked how they reacted to my politics. I guess the subject never came up because that year, when I turned twenty-one and registered to vote as a Democrat, they were shocked.

One afternoon, Ed's brother brought in the mail and reluctantly handed me a letter from the New York State Democratic Committee. "This is the first piece of Democratic mail ever to be delivered to this house," he solemnly announced. That day, I realized that both of our families were dealing with a revolutionary concept. At that point, Ed and I vowed never to discuss religion or politics with either family. I promised to wear my KENNEDY FOR PRESIDENT button only when visiting my folks.

Over the years, many lively political discussions have been held at our kitchen table, with Ed coming down in favor of big business and me championing more programs for the poor. I must confess that I have, on occasion, voted for a Republican and Ed for a Democrat.

One day, soon after our oldest daughter began working, she was having lunch with friends from her office. One of them asked, "Paula, who are your parents voting for in the upcoming election?" She responded, "My dad is voting for George Bush, and my mom is voting for Bill Clinton." Her friends were shocked. "You must be mistaken, Paula. Wives don't vote for different candidates than their husbands." Being the product of a "mixed marriage," I found this remark quite funny. "Maybe in your family they don't, but in my family, my parents often vote for opposing candidates. Besides, you obviously don't know my mom very well, do you?"

In 2000, I was watching the Democratic convention when new friends of ours dropped by for a visit. "You're watching the Democratic convention?" one of them asked in horror. "Of course," I answered. "We watch both conventions. How do you know what each party stands for if you don't watch both conventions? Besides, Ed's the Republican in this family. I'm a Democrat." Over the years, Ed and I have enjoyed watching our friends' reactions when we reveal that we are from opposite sides of the aisle. Our new friends just looked confused.

In recent years, our political beliefs have become more alike. We both want this terrible war to end; we worry about the talk of overturning *Roe* v. *Wade*; and we believe that outsourcing jobs has had a disastrous effect on our economy. We fear that government has begun to assume the role of religion: embracing all the taboos and restrictions, but not the virtues of charity and compassion.

In September 2009, Ed and I will have been married fifty years. Life certainly has been exciting and interesting. We raised four wonderful children who watch both parties' political conventions and are far more open-minded than their parents' families. I believe we are living proof that Donkeys and Elephants can coexist, even in the institution of marriage. I guess the moral is that with enough love and a heavy dose of humor, you truly can live happily ever after.

Barbara Ann Carle

Discovery

After I collected my luggage, I looked frantically around the airport for a phone to call my college and get directions to the campus. Long before the cell phone came along, phone booths existed. Not anymore. (I wonder what Superman does now.)

Excited, sleep-deprived, and running on adrenaline, I couldn't wait to meet my roommates from all over the world.

Deciding to join Friends World College (FWC) instead of going to Annapolis as my parents had hoped was my first big independent decision and the start of changes that rocked my family. The name of my college pretty much said what its focus was as a higher educational institution: to help build community by having students emerge themselves in different countries around the globe. We were to become friends of the world. Students were required to spend every year in a different country on projects they designed themselves, while they learned the language and culture. As an aspiring photographer who grew up absorbed in the pages of *National Geographic* and *Life* magazines, I was enthralled by my school's ideals.

Finally, someone answered the phone casually. "Yes? You're at the airport? Yes? Then take the next Long Island Limo to Huntington. See ya."

A limousine? I thought. *He can't mean a limousine, can he? That would cost me a fortune.* How was I supposed to know that there was a limo-shuttle service from JFK to Long Island? I guess I could have asked, but I was feeling alone and insecure.

I felt a hand on my shoulder. "Taxi?" smiled a cab driver with gaps between his gleaming front teeth.

After a ride that seemed to last longer than the airplane trip—mainly because I asked too many questions about the driver's home country—I bit my lip and paid the fee. I had just $200—the only funds my father decided to put toward my education after disowning me for not going to Annapolis or an art college.

"So you're the one that took a taxi from JFK?" I was later asked by Bob Rodriguez, my faculty advisor. Bob had a degree from Columbia and worked at FWC part-time. He looked after the Latino students like me. "Saw your portfolio. It's impressive. How'd you like to work on the Kennedy campaign?"

"Ted Kennedy?"

"Yeah. Ted's running for president. You're a registered Democrat, aren't you?"

"No," I said.

"We'll fix that," he assured me. "You are a Democrat, aren't you?"

"I don't know. Am I?"

"I've seen your portfolio, remember?" he said, raising his eyebrows.

"Yeah," I said, scratching my head.

"Well, then, you're a Democrat."

That was the beginning—or at least what I remember—of being introduced to the Democrats. I had grown up in a strict Republican household where "those people" were never discussed. When I asked Bob why my photographs showed that I was a Democrat, he answered simply, "There's one photo that will stay in my mind forever. It was a homeless girl living in a ruined church in Colombia.

She was dressed in dirty rags that hung from her emaciated body. Her shoes were torn in two, and a tear was forming in one eye . . . And you ask 'why'?"

"Yes," I answered in all honesty, never having been involved in politics before.

"Well, a Republican would have taken a photo of the ruined church only, and not any of the homeless children living inside it." That was Bob—matter of fact. And it was because of Bob that I found myself on the floor of Madison Square Garden photographing President Carter at the 1979 Democratic National Convention. After Ted Kennedy's failed attempt to become the democratic candidate for president, I was hired as a photographer for the Hispanic American Democrats (HAD)—yes, I know they have changed their name—to photograph President Carter. Ten months after landing at JFK, I was totally wrapped up in a presidential election.

As the president gave his address, I took photo after photo, hoping to capture the electric atmosphere in the Garden. That sensation wasn't because of Carter alone; it was being generated by the audience as well. Ted Kennedy had rocked the Garden the night before as tears streamed down the faces of women and men. I couldn't help but be amazed at the emotions I witnessed. Looking into the eyes of an elderly woman as she hung onto every word Kennedy spoke made it almost impossible to focus the camera. She brought tears to my eyes.

This early experience of working within a large community of Democrats representing every state, to help elect an individual who would bring about positive change for the American people, brought me into politics. I've never looked back. It also permanently severed my relationship with my parents.

Excitedly, I had phoned my father from the Garden that day to tell him the news that I had photographed the president. I remember the conversation well.

"Carter?" he asked sarcastically.

"Yes, Dad, the president," I responded, bewildered at his tone.

"How could you?" he asked. I had no reply. I honestly thought he would be proud. "Don't you know he's a Democrat?" he said.

"Sure, I know," I answered.

"When will you grow up?" he sighed, and there was an eternal dead space on the phone. I couldn't find anything to say. All I was interested in was getting back to the convention—where I could hear cheers still emanating from the convention floor. The sound rolled in waves from a united people who had formed their own family that I was now proud to be a part of.

"Are you still there?" my father asked.

A part of me just wanted to hang up, but I answered, "Yeah, I'm here."

"When are you going to stop this foolishness?"

I didn't answer.

"I've had just about enough from you, young lady. Don't bother coming home until you get your priorities in line," he commanded.

"I'm home now," I said, and I found the courage to hang up the phone.

Ramona du Houx

Democrat Versus Republican

The first Presidential election that I can recall was Eisenhower versus Stevenson. I remember walking between my mother and father, solemnly holding their hands as we made our way to the elementary school where they cast their votes for Adlai Stevenson. Apparently, they did not like Ike all that much. Since both my parents were devout Democrats, that was not exactly a surprise.

"What are we doing?" I asked my parents.

"Your daddy and I are voting for the president of the United States. It's one of the most important things we can do as citizens and a real privilege." My mother's expression was serious. I understood that they were doing something really important that day. I never forgot it.

Coming from a working-class background, I expected all my relatives voted Democratic as well. But soon after the election, while attending a family circle, I was in for a rude awakening.

My mother had three sisters who were very close. The women were in the kitchen cleaning up dishes when my father and my favorite uncle got into a heated debate in the parlor over politics. This was particularly surprising as my father was normally the quietest of people. My mother and aunt, on hearing the raised voices of their husbands, exchanged looks and headed straight back to the kitchen without further comment. However, being an inquisitive child, I had other ideas and eavesdropped on their conversation.

"Thank the Lord, Ike won the election," my uncle was saying. "Now the country won't be controlled by fascists and communists anymore. Finally, we'll have prosperity again." (*I like Ike* was the winning campaign slogan.)

This was pure provocation for my father, who ground down on his back molars. "I guess you've forgotten how it was when the Republicans shoved us into the Depression in the first place. Why, if it wasn't for FDR, we would all have starved to death." My dad worshipped Franklin Delano Roosevelt as if he were a deity, just the way my mother adored Eleanor Roosevelt and fervently believed she was the greatest woman who had ever lived.

I heard my uncle choking on his coffee. "Roosevelt? Don't mention that man's name in my house," he said. "Why, that viper tried to pack the Supreme Court! He's responsible for the Russians gobbling up half of Europe. That's what the Democrats did for us."

Dad was on his feet now. As far as he was concerned, attacking Roosevelt was nothing short of sacrilege. "I suppose you think you're one of those rich men who support the Republicans!"

My uncle stood up as well, and they faced each other like two gunfighters at high noon. I half expected them to begin circling each other and pull out six-shooters. Everyone else had the good sense to leave the room, not wanting to get caught in the crossfire.

"I know I'm not rich," my uncle asserted, "but I do work for myself. I don't see why I should have to pay Social Security when I could invest that money and make it grow." My uncle's face turned a shade of red comparable to a rare roast beef. "You Democrats want the government to control everyone's life. I'm a Republican because I believe in freedom for the individual."

"You mean laissez-faire capitalism, don't you?"

"That government governs best that governs least," my uncle quoted.

"What's good for big business is good for America?" My father jutted his jaw. He was a factory worker, part of the labor force that believed in the rights of working men and supported strong labor unions. "Well, unlike Republicans, Democrats care about the underdog."

My uncle frowned at my father. "Republicans have integrity. We're not looking for government handouts. We work hard and don't take relief or welfare."

"You're saying Democrats don't have integrity?" Dad countered. "Well, you're wrong. What about Truman? Give 'em hell Harry? The man who said, 'The buck stops here.' He didn't take garbage from anybody."

My uncle shrugged. "Ike was a great general, a war hero like George Washington. He's going to be great for this country. You can have Truman!"

The argument finally ended in a draw. Neither my dad nor my uncle could convince the other. They were both stubborn and entrenched in their political viewpoints, like two pit bulls. But by tacit consent, they never argued politics again. They knew it was a waste of time and effort. They simply agreed to disagree.

I learned a lot that day. It was a turning point in my life. I began thinking for myself. I loved and respected both my father and my uncle. They were both fine men. And although I've leaned Democratic to this day, I don't just vote the party line. I always look for candidates who'll do the best job for the country regardless of party affiliation. And I will and do vote Republican if I believe that party is providing the better candidate.

I try to stay informed. It's a privilege to live in a country where people can express conflicting opinions and ideas. Some of our best legislation and ideas for social reform have come from third parties or independents. In that regard, the Democrats are usually more receptive, quicker to adopt and accept ideas that originate with independents, the way FDR did with what were considered radical socialist reforms during the Depression. It's important to be open to progressive thinking. Yes, I have to admit, I will always tend to lean toward the Democratic viewpoint.

Jacqueline Seewald

Pressing the Flesh

My aunt was a big woman. She was as wide as a hundred-year-old tree trunk. She had flashing eyes and a high-pitched laugh that echoed through the hallways of Anthony's Seafood Grotto in San Diego, her favorite haunt. Little finger lifted, she would slurp her salty oysters and slam a clam or six down her ample gullet. My Aunt Zella loved to eat.

She was married to skinny Uncle Ray. He was a crunchy cracker of a man who hailed from Arkansas and delighted in getting my eyes wider than a barn owl's with his stories. He'd tell me how he got shot through with buckshot, and how they took out his whole intestine and slapped some "ce-ment" in the holes, twisted the whole mess together, and stuck it back in his gut to make the man that he was that day, sitting in front of me—little black-eyed Susie, six years old.

Uncle Ray owned a cement factory, and that's where we would visit them, in El Cajon, in the dusty yard, sleeping in the prefab trailer, where we vacationed in the sun and mud, and my mother wondered where the glamour was in California.

Aunt Zella was my father's baby sister. She cut her toenails with pinking shears and polished her fingernails with red paint. She was also a passionate, lifelong Democrat. In 1956, she was chairperson for Adlai Stevenson and Estes Kefauver in the state of California. She hated Tricky Dick and made it a ritual for us still-Jewish flat-landers from the Midwest to answer her questions daily.

"Who will ruin the American government?"

"Richard Nixon, Aunt Zella."

"Who is worse than the communists?"

Democrat's Soul

"Richard Nixon, Aunt Zella."

"Who will you never vote for as long as you live?"

"Richard Nixon, Aunt Zella!"

"Mark my words, the man is unstable!"

She would then steer her mound of fervent flesh away from the fence post where I was perched with her rangy sons and my red-haired siblings, and rustle back toward her dusty office.

Our job that summer in El Cajon was to load and reload campaign signs into the back of Uncle Ray's pickup. Zella would get all dressed up in her light silk sheath, impossibly high heels, and clouds of racy perfume. She would carefully spray her short hair away from her face, make sure her nails were red and flawless, paint on her eyebrows, and tiptoe through the dust to the truck. We'd get into the back of the flatbed and she'd roar out of the cement yard, with us holding onto our hats and the smiling pictures of Stevenson and Kefauver.

Soon we'd hit the cooler streets of San Diego. The breeze from the water would find us, lift our hair off our sweaty necks and soothe our skin. We lounged at the ready as Aunt Zella rallied supporters in this church or that factory basement. When it was time, we'd bring in the signs and make sure everyone had one for their lawn.

Afterwards, we'd head to Anthony's Seafood Grotto for an afternoon plate of fried shrimp and Cokes. Zella would tell us about how Stevenson and Kefauver were going to save the country. She would make the waitresses and the bus boys sit with us and eat and drink. She would tell them how we kids were going to benefit, how we would grow up and know all kinds of people and learn all kinds of things as long as we studied hard and got smart. That's how she escaped her Canadian, Depression-era background, she told us. And she told us in Spanish, Yiddish, Arkansas cracker, and the King's English.

Aunt Zella never lost faith. She believed that a kid, like her, who had gone for a week with nothing more than a piece of bread and a cup of tea, deserved to be the fattest woman in the county. She believed in the power of smart people with open hearts to support the little guy, and she believed in the freedom of poor people to rise from the wintry plains of Winnipeg, Manitoba, where she was born, to the elite of southern California politics.

My father's family was like that. They were passionate, idealistic, and willing to fight the good fight. There were the fat ones like Zella and the skinny, crazy ones like my other aunt, who worked for the *Chicago Sun-Times* and wrote crusading editorials against the big business interests in her town. And there were the lost ones, like my aunt Bea, who lived for years in a little apartment in New York City. At her death, she left behind little more than a Ponytail autograph book full of political cartoons from the *New Yorker* and a dusty copy of Zella's picture from a San Diego newspaper announcing her baby sister's elevation to state chairperson.

My family believed that it was possible to change the world. They had seen their world in bits and pieces through the cracked lens of the Depression and World War II, and they still believed. And even though Bobby Kennedy was a fascist and worked with Roy Cohn, a fallen-away Jew who disgraced the name of all immigrant dreamers, they still believed that the real Democrats, the poor ones with faces of different colors and dirty nails and great hearts—the union workers from my town and the "colored" people moving north and the Mexicans building a better life—that all those people were part of a real America, an America that we all had a stake in. And they believed that none of the real guys had names like Rockefeller or Ike.

I remember the idealism of my odd and prescient family, and their belief in this country and its Democratic Party. I trace that same allegiance, which I now hold dear, to Zella's roly-poly lifted finger and the certainty that there is room for everyone at the table.

Susan Merson

Democrat's Soul

off the mark.com   by Mark Parisi

USUALLY, I HAND-COUNT EVERYBODY'S CHRISTMAS LIST, BUT THIS YEAR I GOT A DEAL ON SOME TABULATION MACHINES FROM FLORIDA...

ATLANTIC FEATURE © 2000 MARK PARISI

offthemark.com

WH[donkey] SAID IT?

"What this country
needs is a good
five-cent cigar."
—*Thomas R. Marshall*

"Always vote for principle,
though you may vote alone,
and you may cherish the sweetest
reflection that your vote is never lost."
—*John Quincy Adams*

"You ain't learnin'
nothin' when
you're talkin'.
—*Lyndon B. Johnson*

"Republicans are men of narrow
vision, who are afraid
of the future."
—*Jimmy Carter*

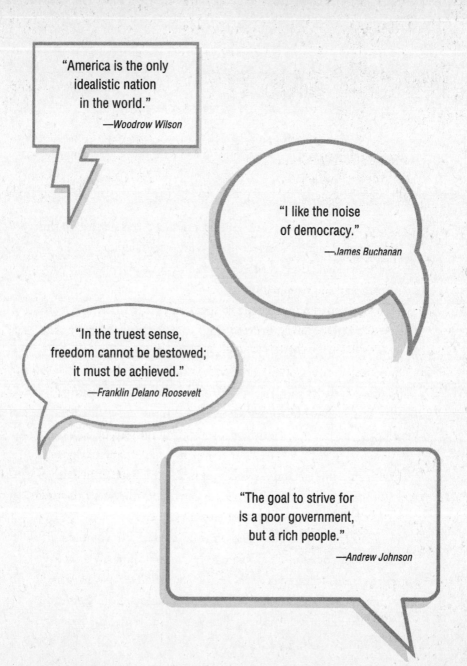

"America is the only idealistic nation in the world."
—Woodrow Wilson

"I like the noise of democracy."
—James Buchanan

"In the truest sense, freedom cannot be bestowed; it must be achieved."
—Franklin Delano Roosevelt

"The goal to strive for is a poor government, but a rich people."
—Andrew Johnson

Franklin Delano Roosevelt
First Inaugural Address, Delivered March 4, 1933

President Hoover, Mr. Chief Justice, my friends:

This is a day of national consecration. And I am certain that on this day my fellow Americans expect that on my induction into the Presidency, I will address them with a candor and a decision which the present situation of our people impels.

This is preeminently the time to speak the truth, the whole truth, frankly and boldly. Nor need we shrink from honestly facing conditions in our country today. This great Nation will endure, as it has endured, will revive and will prosper.

So, first of all, let me assert my firm belief that the only thing we have to fear is fear itself—nameless, unreasoning, unjustified terror which paralyzes needed efforts to convert retreat into advance. In every dark hour of our national life, a leadership of frankness and of vigor has met with that understanding and support of the people themselves which is essential to victory. And I am convinced that you will again give that support to leadership in these critical days.

In such a spirit on my part and on yours we face our common difficulties. They concern, thank God, only material things. Values have shrunk to fantastic levels; taxes have risen; our ability to pay has fallen; government of all kinds is faced by serious curtailment of income; the means of exchange are frozen in the currents of trade; the withered leaves of industrial enterprise lie on every side; farmers find no markets for their produce; and the savings of many years in thousands of families are gone. More important, a host of unemployed citizens face the grim problem of existence, and an equally great number toil with little return. Only a foolish optimist can deny the dark realities of the moment.

And yet our distress comes from no failure of substance. We are stricken by no plague of locusts. Compared with the perils which our forefathers conquered, because they believed and were not afraid, we have still much to be thankful for. Nature still offers her bounty and human efforts have multiplied it. Plenty is at our doorstep, but a generous use of it languishes in the very sight of the supply.

Primarily, this is because the rulers of the exchange of mankind's goods have failed, through their own stubbornness and their own incompetence, have admitted their failure, and have abdicated. Practices of the unscrupulous money changers stand indicted in the court of public opinion, rejected by the hearts and minds of men.

True, they have tried. But their efforts have been cast in the pattern of an outworn tradition. Faced by failure of credit, they have proposed only the lending of more money. Stripped of the lure of profit by which to induce our people to follow their false leadership, they have resorted to exhortations, pleading tearfully for restored confidence. They only know the rules of a generation of self-seekers. They have no vision, and when there is no vision the people perish.

Yes, the money changers have fled from their high seats in the temple of our civilization. We may now restore that temple to the ancient truths. The measure of that restoration lies in the extent to which we apply social values more noble than mere monetary profit.

Happiness lies not in the mere possession of money; it lies in the joy of achievement, in the thrill of creative effort. The joy, the moral stimulation of work no longer must be forgotten in the mad chase of evanescent profits. These dark days, my friends, will be worth all they cost us if they teach us that our true destiny is not to be ministered unto but to minister to ourselves, to our fellow men.

Recognition of that falsity of material wealth as the standard of success goes hand in hand with the abandonment of the false belief that public office and high political position are to be valued only by the standards of pride of place and personal profit; and there must be an end to a conduct in banking and in business which too often has given to a sacred trust the likeness of callous and selfish wrongdoing. Small wonder that confidence languishes, for it thrives only on honesty, on honor, on the sacredness of obligations, on faithful protection, and on unselfish performance; without them it cannot live.

Restoration calls, however, not for changes in ethics alone. This Nation is asking for action, and action now.

Our greatest primary task is to put people to work. This is no unsolvable problem if we face it wisely and courageously. It can be accomplished in part by direct recruiting by the Government itself, treating the task as we would treat the emergency of a war, but at the same time, through this employment, accomplishing great—greatly needed projects to stimulate and reorganize the use of our great natural resources.

Hand in hand with that we must frankly recognize the overbalance of population in our industrial centers and, by engaging on a national scale in a redistribution, endeavor to provide a better use of the land for those best fitted for the land.

Yes, the task can be helped by definite efforts to raise the values of agricultural products, and with this the power to purchase the output of our cities. It can be helped by preventing realistically the tragedy of the growing loss through foreclosure of our small homes and our farms. It can be helped by insistence that the Federal, the State, and the local governments act forthwith on the demand that their cost be drastically reduced. It can be helped by the unifying of relief activities which today are often scattered, uneconomical, unequal. It can be helped by national planning for and supervision of all forms of transportation and of communications and other utilities that have a definitely public character. There are many ways in which it can be helped, but it can never be helped by merely talking about it.

We must act. We must act quickly.

And finally, in our progress towards a resumption of work, we require two safeguards against a return of the evils of the old order. There must be a strict supervision of all banking and credits and investments. There must be an end to speculation with other people's money. And there must be provision for an adequate but sound currency.

These, my friends, are the lines of attack. I shall presently urge upon a new Congress in special session detailed measures for their fulfillment, and I shall seek the immediate assistance of the 48 States.

Through this program of action we address ourselves to putting our own national house in order and making income balance outgo. Our international trade relations, though vastly important, are in point of time, and necessity, secondary to the establishment of a sound national economy. I favor, as a practical policy, the putting of first things first. I shall spare no effort to restore world trade by international economic readjustment; but the emergency at home cannot wait on that accomplishment.

The basic thought that guides these specific means of national recovery is not nationally—narrowly nationalistic. It is the insistence, as a first consideration, upon the interdependence of the various elements in and parts of the United States of America—a recognition of the old and permanently important manifestation of the American spirit of the pioneer. It is the way to recovery. It is the immediate way. It is the strongest assurance that recovery will endure.

In the field of world policy, I would dedicate this Nation to the policy of the good neighbor: the neighbor who resolutely respects himself and, because he does so, respects the rights of others; the neighbor who respects his obligations and respects the sanctity of his agreements in and with a world of neighbors.

If I read the temper of our people correctly, we now realize, as we have never realized before, our interdependence on each other; that we can not merely take, but we must give as well; that if we are to go forward, we must move as a trained and loyal army willing to sacrifice for the good of a common discipline, because without such discipline no progress can be made, no leadership becomes effective.

We are, I know, ready and willing to submit our lives and our property to such discipline, because it makes possible a leadership which aims at the larger good. This, I propose to offer, pledging that the larger purposes will bind upon us, bind upon us all as a sacred obligation with a unity of duty hitherto evoked only in times of armed strife.

With this pledge taken, I assume unhesitatingly the leadership of this great army of our people dedicated to a disciplined attack upon our common problems.

Action in this image, action to this end is feasible under the form of government which we have inherited from our ancestors. Our Constitution is so simple, so practical that it is possible always to meet extraordinary needs by changes in emphasis and arrangement without loss of essential form. That is why our constitutional system has proved itself the most superbly enduring political mechanism the modern world has ever seen.

It has met every stress of vast expansion of territory, of foreign wars, of bitter internal strife, of world relations. And it is to be hoped that the normal balance of executive and legislative authority may be wholly equal, wholly adequate to meet the unprecedented task before us. But it may be that an unprecedented demand and need for undelayed action may call for temporary departure from that normal balance of public procedure.

I am prepared under my constitutional duty to recommend the measures that a stricken nation in the midst of a stricken world may require. These measures, or such other measures as the Congress may build out of its experience and wisdom, I shall seek, within my constitutional authority, to bring to speedy adoption.

But, in the event that the Congress shall fail to take one of these two courses, in the event that the national emergency is still critical, I shall not evade the clear course of duty that will then confront me. I shall ask the Congress for the one remaining instrument to meet the crisis—broad Executive power to wage a war against the emergency, as great as the power that would be given to me if we were in fact invaded by a foreign foe.

For the trust reposed in me, I will return the courage and the devotion that befit the time. I can do no less.

We face the arduous days that lie before us in the warm courage of national unity; with the clear consciousness of seeking old and precious moral values; with the clean satisfaction that comes from the stern performance of duty by old and young alike. We aim at the assurance of a rounded, a permanent national life.

We do not distrust the—the future of essential democracy. The people of the United States have not failed. In their need they have registered a mandate that they want direct, vigorous action. They have asked for discipline and direction under leadership. They have made me the present instrument of their wishes. In the spirit of the gift I take it.

In this dedication—In this dedication of a Nation, we humbly ask the blessing of God.

May He protect each and every one of us.

May He guide me in the days to come.

A great moment in Democratic history: President Franklin Delano Roosevelt is joined by Winston Churchill and Joseph Stalin at the Yalta Conference in February 1945. FDR gained Stalin's support for the new United Nations and for participating in the US Pacific War against Japan after the defeat of Nazi Germany.

Trivia

1. Who was the first woman to serve in the Cabinet?

2. What was the largest number of ballots needed to nominate a Democratic presidential candidate?

3. Who was the Democratic candidate who lost the most races for the presidency?

4. Which two Democrats became president after serving as vice president to a man of a different party?

5. When did a non-Democrat run for the presidency as the nominee of the Democratic Party?

6. What Democratic candidates for the presidency won the popular vote, but lost in the Electoral College?

7. Who was the only man to run unsuccessfully for vice president and subsequently be elected president?

8. Who was the first First Lady to win elective office?

9. Who was the first senator directly elected by the people?

10. Who was the first African-American mayor of a major American city?

1. Frances Perkins, Secretary of Labor 1933–1945

2. In 1924 it took 103 ballots to nominate John W. Davis

3. William Jennings Bryan, the "Great Commoner," who ran in 1896, 1900, and 1908

4. John Tyler in 1841, after the death of William Henry Harrison, and Andrew Johnson in 1865, after the assassination of Abraham Lincoln

5. Horace Greeley, a Liberal Republican, in 1872

6. Samuel Tilden in 1876, Grover Cleveland in 1888, and Albert Gore in 2000

7. Franklin Delano Roosevelt, who was James M. Cox's running mate in 1920, and who was elected president in 1932

8. Hillary Clinton, elected senator from New York in 2000

9. Augustus O. Bacon of Georgia following passage of the XVIIth Amendment in 1913

10. Carl Stokes, Mayor of Cleveland, Ohio, 1965–1973

R.E.S.P.E.C.T.

After my seventeen-year marriage ended in divorce, my goal was to concentrate on my career in financial management and to make certain my son got into a good college. I had no interest in dating, and I vowed "I'll never marry again."

Four months passed, and I was settling in. Life was good being a single mom and raising my sixteen-year-old son. However, lo and behold, my life took an unexpected turn.

One afternoon, I had an appointment with a customer who was interested in obtaining an equity loan. My heart leapt when he walked into my office and introduced himself.

"I'm Nolan," he said. I couldn't help but stare as he readily poured himself a cup of coffee from a silver carafe I kept on a lateral file cabinet near my desk. His thick, fiery red hair fascinated me, as well as his impish grin and the bronze freckles scattered across his nose.

I tried my best to be professional as we discussed the real-estate properties he owned, why he needed the money, and what was required to apply for the loan. But I found myself blushing many times during our meeting. I wondered why I was acting like such an adolescent. At the end of the meeting, I shook Nolan's hand and thanked him for his business. I struggled to keep my composure, but it was too late. I heard myself giggling and accepting his invitation to meet him for coffee on Saturday morning.

Over coffee we shared remnants of our lives. He, too, was divorced and shared custody of a son. It didn't take long before we realized we enjoyed one another's company and had a lot in common—except for two things: he was a Republican, and I was a Democrat. Could these differences really matter? As we finished our coffee, I knew I was smitten, and so was he.

A year later, we were married. Marital bliss began with a blended family that consisted of our two sons, our two political parties, moving into a new house, and having a new designated polling place.

The year 1980 was our first Presidential election as a married couple. It was comical to see our mailbox stuffed with Ronald Reagan's Republican campaign literature and Jimmy Carter's Democratic campaign literature. The piles of mail we received from our political parties became a contest. Who'd receive the most mail each day? On most days, I won. "Wow, you Democrats sure like spending money," Nolan teased good-naturedly.

During our thirty years of marriage, we voted in more local, primary, and general elections in the state of California than I can recall. Our polling place was always at our neighborhood firehouse. After we cast our ballots, we'd walk home hand in hand, taking it in stride, knowing we'd more than likely canceled out each other's votes.

In 2000, I must admit I had high hopes for my party. I hung in there, eagerly waiting for the hanging chads to prevail. After the loss, Nolan gave me a hug and made a toast: "There's always 2004."

In 2003, we relocated to the state of Nevada due to Nolan's job being eliminated in California. We made certain we registered to vote in our new state of residence. We made no changes in our party affiliations. Sadly, my Democratic party lost in 2004. Again, we made a toast: "There's always 2008."

On Saturday, January 19, 2008, Nolan and I were elated to be participating in our first presidential caucuses. The news media announced that sites for the Nevada Republican and Democratic caucuses would be high schools, community centers, casinos, and cowboy bars. Gone were the days of casting our ballots at a neighborhood firehouse. We opted for the cowboy bar, but were told it wasn't in our precinct.

Our mailbox began to overflow with Democratic and Republican flyers and leaflets informing us that Nolan's Republican caucus would be held at 9:00 AM in a nearby high school, and my Democratic caucus would be held at 11:00 AM in the neighborhood community center.

After we attended our individual caucuses, we compared notes. As usual, lively, fun-filled banter ensued. He felt his Republican caucus was too chaotic. I thought my Democratic caucus was well organized. We agreed a primary election is better than a caucus and disagreed on who should be in the White House in 2008.

"I'm starving," Nolan said as we finished our feisty repartee.

"I'm not hungry at all," I said. "I had a large banana muffin and coffee at the caucus."

"Are you kidding me?" Nolan asked. "We didn't have anything to drink or eat at my caucus."

I smiled, and then replied, "I rest my case. Democrats rule!"

The only way to explain how we've had a harmonious two-party marriage for thirty years . . . Aretha Franklin says it best: "R.E.S.P.E.C.T."

Georgia A. Hubley

From Red to Blue: How I Became a Democrat

I used to be a Republican. I considered myself strong and independent. I imagined that I could control my life and that everyone else could control theirs, too. I thought that being an American meant being self-sufficient, autonomous, and resolute. I thought that those in need of help were weak, or otherwise flawed. Then I changed my mind.

I was raised in a union home, and mine was a Democrat family. My family didn't get involved in politics beyond voting and heated backyard discussions. After all, it was the 1960s, and civil rights and the Vietnam War made for great barbecue bickering. I was too young to be involved in politics, and I really didn't pay much attention to the specifics. Like most kids, I just assumed that my family had the right views.

When I was seventeen, I enlisted in the Marines. By my nineteenth birthday, I had circumnavigated the globe. I learned a lot in those first few years, and the biggest lesson I learned was how to be responsible for myself. In fact, that's why I became a Republican.

In the Corps, personal responsibility was drummed into my head day after day. Over and over again, I was told the same thing: "You are responsible for everything you do, and everything you fail to do." I was constantly reprimanded for things I'd done, and for those I'd failed to do. It didn't take long for me to believe that I *was* solely responsible for how my life turned out.

Although we were encouraged to vote, politics were never discussed in the Marine Corps. Our officers were very clear—it was unprofessional for them to influence us in any way. They wouldn't even tell us their party affiliations. The leader/subordinate relationship was too important to risk on something as unimportant as politics.

I may not have been subjected to overt political influence, but I *was* influenced nonetheless: my political views changed. I became very conservative. My newfound sense of responsibility affected the way I looked at other people, and also how I looked at political issues. If I was responsible for everything that I did (and failed to do), then it seemed reasonable, even obvious, that everyone else was, too. This thinking left very little room for life's uncertainties: recessions, layoffs, natural disasters, and ordinary, everyday bad luck.

That's how I became a Republican. I gravitated to the party that said what I felt: personal responsibility was the American way. No handouts, no help, and pull yourself up by your bootstraps.

I began to think that everyone was getting what they deserved. Broke? Work harder and make more money. Dead-end job? Go to school, improve yourself. Unemployed? Get a job—the want ads are full of them. Homeless? Get a job, save money, and straighten yourself out. I felt like I had all the answers, and they were always about individual choices. I was very self-righteous about my political points of view.

I stayed in the Marines for a long time. I traveled the world over and over again. I went to a lot of places, and helped a lot of people: oppressed people, poor people, and victims of natural disasters. It never occurred to me that I was providing the very help that I looked down on. I was, in fact, a tool in the execution of social programs, though I didn't see it that way; I was too busy believing that we—the United States—were saving the world.

Two decades later, I returned to civilian life and settled into a regular neighborhood as a regular guy. I got a regular job and began a regular day-to-day routine. I faced regular problems. I spent my days with regular people. In short, I had left the structured, insulated lifestyle of the Marines, and I had entered the wide-open, less predictable lifestyle of John Q. Public. I was no longer in a world of absolutes; I had been thrust into a world filled with gray areas.

I began to see things differently in the world of gray. I learned that even prudent, responsible people needed help sometimes. I saw bad things happen to good people. I saw a hardworking man lose first his job and then his home. I watched illness devour a family's life savings. I watched families search for shelter after their homes had been destroyed by a hurricane. I learned that social programs don't necessarily mean handouts. I learned that needing help wasn't a personal flaw or a sign of weakness.

I had changed. I had become a Democrat—not because Republicans are bad, or even because Democrats are better, but because my philosophies had changed. I had become a different person, and that changed the way I looked at others. I no longer viewed those in need as being weak or otherwise flawed; I stopped seeing social programs as handouts.

Some of my friends say that I've softened over time. Others say that I've finally come to my senses. I say they're all wrong.

I believe in the two-party system. I think our society needs balance, and that no single philosophy, or party, should rule unopposed. But, for now, for this part of my life, I'm going to be a little less conservative. I'm going to be a Democrat.

D. C. Hall

A Rising Tide: My Values and Hopes as a Democrat

I made the decision to be a Democrat during the 2000 presidential election, when my eighth-grade class put on a schoolwide mock election. Each student's vote counted toward a popular vote and toward their class "electoral college" number, which emulated the scoring system of state delegates in the real election. I was one of three leaders from the eighth-grade class to campaign on behalf of the presidential candidates. I chose to "run" for Al Gore.

To my satisfaction, Al Gore had an astounding victory in our school's election, in both popular and electoral votes. The students were impressed by the energetic atmosphere of the campaigns. Our young voters' perspective of politics differed from the national prototype. Without the scrutiny of campaign trails or fundraising tactics, they perceived that all candidates were on equal footing, all were equally qualified to be president, and all were able to carry out their campaign promises in earnest. As fledglings in politics, the students were fortunate to be outside the sphere of national biases as they experienced how political values matched their own basic life values.

We students especially envisioned how educational policy affected our lives and our futures. I began dipping my toes into my own uncharted "liberal" waters when I promoted the Democratic educational policy. I explained how my party would improve public schools by providing more money to school districts that needed to make improvements, and by providing better pay for teachers, who could extend extra help to students. My opponent's campaign for George W. Bush described a policy that would grant more money as a reward to the schools that were already in good condition, and provide a "charter school" option to individuals who wanted their children to move into a better district. My opponent's policy sounded irresponsible to me—it avoided change in the neglected places where change was needed most. My liberal values, like a rising tide, began to take shape.

I was a high school senior during the 2004 presidential election. As I prepared for my future, the prospect of changes in my life reminded me of the power of developing my potential. I, like many of my peers, was skeptical about the Iraq war and its political atmosphere, and having just turned eighteen, I voted for John Kerry. I delighted at the possibility that my vote could move the government in a new direction. I was hopeful about the future, not only for my country, but for reaching personal fulfillment.

Since then I have tried to be proactive in my personal and political lives, which increasingly overlap. As a Democrat, or a liberal, I have been called irresponsible, even lazy, by the irreverent voices of right-wing personalities over the radio on cold morning drives to my college campus. Yet at school I make an effort to apply myself "liberally," because to be liberal means to gain by giving, to learn by doing. I am liberal when I seek guidance from my teachers with initiative, effort, and appreciation toward learning. I am increasingly satisfied as I become more apt at meeting change and staking a claim in the bounty of change. When I meet change proactively, I have access to new knowledge and new opportunities.

I have struggled to create expectations for myself: What are my unexplored talents? What are my unhatched ideas? What have I left behind? I have worked to mend the wings of dreams, broken by my own reckless neglect. I have enriched my life by pulling my spirit out of self-doubt, by directing positive light into neglected corners of my personality, and by maintaining a strong sense of self who can anticipate the challenges and seize the opportunities that I will encounter. I expect a government to strive no less toward achieving its goals. An exemplary liberal government will identify and utilize strengths, seek and create solutions, set new expectations, and encourage development wherever there has been too little development in our nation.

In 2000, during my mock election campaign, I viewed the Democratic Party as the government of outreach, public participation, and political proactivity. My classmate and opponent, on behalf of the Republican Party, campaigned on the values of lower taxes, privacy and security, and freedom with less involvement from government.

"If the citizens do not participate, how can we say we live in a democracy?" I objected.

"We don't. We live in a republic," was my opponent's reply.

I realized that politics was not only a measure of opinion, but a whole attitude toward life, and a test of each of our inner values and strengths.

Politicians refer to spending money as making national investments. From a monetary perspective I see it this way: whether Democrat or Republican, our politicians are paid by our taxes. Why not pay the person who will do the most work at developing the nation in which we invest our lives, our money, and our happiness? In a democracy, we value the two-way investments between ourselves and our government. We hold the keys to our government's resources, because we are the suppliers and consumers of health care, education, labor, and manufactured products. A Democratic government helps us fulfill our personal and national potential by a committed investment in the resources we all share.

I envision a national government that works for its people's well-being; that examines the tiny seeds of potential and nourishes their growth out of the dark; that surpasses expectations in creating goals and renewing a sense of hope in the nation. I view our political leaders as navigators of change. I will happily vote for Clinton or Obama in November 2008 because a Democratic president will stand up for change. Change has helped me grow through struggle and toward hope. Our Democratic leaders are with us to guide our nation's strong growth into the bounty of opportunities change will bring.

Brittany Beckman

Getting Along

When my daughter introduced me and my husband to her future in-laws, she whispered in my ear, "Just don't mention politics, Mom."

Uh-oh, I thought. *Are we in for trouble already?*

Future in-laws have a hard enough time trying to figure out how to accept the new family coming into their lives without having prohibitions up front.

I can understand my daughter's caution, however. Generally I am a mild, accepting, gentle person. But bring up certain topics and the mildness turns feisty, the acceptance becomes critical, and the gentle demeanor that those around me find so soothing changes into something forceful, a volcano that overwhelms anyone around me. My daughter knows this about me. She also knows that I grew up in a Democratic household and that I continue my Democratic allegiance. From her warning, nervous glances at her father-in-law-to-be, I guessed that he had a similar attachment to the Republicans. I could see that it might not be a good idea to delve into a political discussion at such an important gathering.

I kept the conversation to more congenial topics throughout dinner—our homes, our careers, where we grew up. We spoke about our travels as we ate, and about our gardens. We discussed the birds that visit our feeders and the squirrels that often outwit our efforts to keep them off the feeders. And we talked about how nicely our families were blending, how happy we were that our children had found each other. As we had our dessert, we made plans for the wedding, and ended the evening feeling that we were compatible.

"There was nothing to worry about," I told my daughter when we were alone. "We are all grown-ups. We know how to get along."

She just smiled and hugged me.

Each time our families got together, my daughter reminded me not to get into politics. I suspected that my future son-in-law made a similar plea to his father who, it seems, had equally strong and often opposite opinions from mine. So we discussed everything else. Whenever the topic skirted a hot subject, our children visibly tensed. Once there was a moment of silence when the matter of how Congress was handling a proposed bill found its way into our conversation. No doubt we would be on opposite sides of the congressional aisle. I saw the caution in my husband's eyes, and I knew the discussion could easily lead to a rift of volcanic proportions in our forming family. So I took a breath and smiled. There was no eruption.

After the wedding, my husband and I were invited to dinner with our new family members. We spent several hours together and talked about many things—but not politics. My son-in-law's father had a good, caring soul, wrapped around a Republican point of view. My outlook on life embraced a Democratic perspective. But it didn't matter. We were determined to get along. We liked each other. We knew that we would be supportive of this marriage and wonderful with any grandchildren who might come along. Whatever our politics, there was common, loving ground here for both of us.

Ferida Wolff

Reprinted by permission of Mark Parisi. ©2008 Mark Parisi.

WHO SAID IT?

"If you can't convince them, confuse them."

—*Harry S. Truman*

"May our country be always successful, but whether successful or otherwise, always right."

—*John Quincy Adams*

"As Americans, we go forward, in the service of our country, by the will of God."

—*Franklin Delano Roosevelt*

"Ask not what your country can do for you; ask what you can do for your country."

—*John F. Kennedy*

Democrat's Soul

"All politics is local."

—*Thomas "Tip" O'Neill*

"If you will think about what you ought to do for other people, your character will take care of itself."

—*Woodrow Wilson*

"There is nothing wrong with America that can't be fixed with what is right in America."

—*William Clinton*

"To act coolly, intelligently, and prudently in perilous circumstances is the test of a man—and also a nation."

—*Adlai Stevenson*

John F. Kennedy
Inaugural Address,
Delivered January 20, 1961

Vice President Johnson, Mr. Speaker, Mr. Chief Justice, President Eisenhower, Vice President Nixon, President Truman, reverend clergy, fellow citizens:

We observe today not a victory of party, but a celebration of freedom—symbolizing an end, as well as a beginning—signifying renewal, as well as change. For I have sworn before you and Almighty God the same solemn oath our forebears prescribed nearly a century and three-quarters ago.

The world is very different now. For man holds in his mortal hands the power to abolish all forms of human poverty and all forms of human life. And yet the same revolutionary beliefs for which our forebears fought are still at issue around the globe—the belief that the rights of man come not from the generosity of the state, but from the hand of God.

We dare not forget today that we are the heirs of that first revolution. Let the word go forth from this time and place, to friend and foe alike, that the torch has been passed to a new generation of Americans—born in this century, tempered by war, disciplined by a hard and bitter peace, proud of our ancient heritage, and unwilling to witness or permit the slow undoing of those human rights to which this nation has always been committed, and to which we are committed today at home and around the world.

Let every nation know, whether it wishes us well or ill, that we shall pay any price, bear any burden, meet any hardship, support any friend, oppose any foe, to assure the survival and the success of liberty.

This much we pledge—and more.

To those old allies whose cultural and spiritual origins we share, we pledge the loyalty of faithful friends. United there is little we cannot do in a host of cooperative ventures. Divided there is little we can do—for we dare not meet a powerful challenge at odds and split asunder.

To those new states whom we welcome to the ranks of the free, we pledge our word that one form of colonial control shall not have passed away merely to be replaced by a far more iron tyranny. We shall not always expect to find them supporting our view. But we shall always hope to find them strongly supporting their own freedom—and to remember that, in the past, those who foolishly sought power by riding the back of the tiger ended up inside.

To those people in the huts and villages of half the globe struggling to break the bonds of mass misery, we pledge our best efforts to help them help themselves, for whatever period is required—not because the Communists may be doing it, not because we seek their votes, but because it is right. If a free society cannot help the many who are poor, it cannot save the few who are rich.

To our sister republics south of our border, we offer a special pledge: to convert our good words into good deeds, in a new alliance for progress, to assist free men and free governments in casting off the chains of poverty. But this peaceful revolution of hope cannot become the prey of hostile powers. Let all our neighbors know that we shall join with them to oppose aggression or subversion anywhere in the Americas. And let every other power know that this hemisphere intends to remain the master of its own house.

To that world assembly of sovereign states, the United Nations, our last best hope in an age where the instruments of war have far outpaced the instruments of peace, we renew our pledge of support—to prevent it from becoming merely a forum for invective, to strengthen its shield of the new and the weak, and to enlarge the area in which its writ may run.

Finally, to those nations who would make themselves our adversary, we offer not a pledge but a request: that both sides begin anew the quest for peace, before the dark powers of destruction unleashed by science engulf all humanity in planned or accidental self-destruction.

We dare not tempt them with weakness. For only when our arms are sufficient beyond doubt can we be certain beyond doubt that they will never be employed.

But neither can two great and powerful groups of nations take comfort from our present course—both sides overburdened by the cost of modern weapons, both rightly alarmed by the steady spread of the deadly atom, yet both racing to alter that uncertain balance of terror that stays the hand of mankind's final war.

So let us begin anew—remembering on both sides that civility is not a sign of weakness, and sincerity is always subject to proof. Let us never negotiate out of fear, but let us never fear to negotiate.

Democrat's Soul

Let both sides explore what problems unite us instead of belaboring those problems which divide us.

Let both sides, for the first time, formulate serious and precise proposals for the inspection and control of arms, and bring the absolute power to destroy other nations under the absolute control of all nations.

Let both sides seek to invoke the wonders of science instead of its terrors. Together let us explore the stars, conquer the deserts, eradicate disease, tap the ocean depths, and encourage the arts and commerce.

Let both sides unite to heed, in all corners of the earth, the command of Isaiah—to "undo the heavy burdens, and [to] let the oppressed go free."

And, if a beachhead of cooperation may push back the jungle of suspicion, let both sides join in creating a new endeavor—not a new balance of power, but a new world of law—where the strong are just, and the weak secure, and the peace preserved.

All this will not be finished in the first one hundred days. Nor will it be finished in the first one thousand days; nor in the life of this Administration; nor even perhaps in our lifetime on this planet. But let us begin.

In your hands, my fellow citizens, more than mine, will rest the final success or failure of our course. Since this country was founded, each generation of Americans has been summoned to give testimony to its national loyalty. The graves of young Americans who answered the call to service surround the globe.

Now the trumpet summons us again—not as a call to bear arms, though arms we need—not as a call to battle, though embattled we are—

but a call to bear the burden of a long twilight struggle, year in and year out, "rejoicing in hope; patient in tribulation," a struggle against the common enemies of man: tyranny, poverty, disease, and war itself.

Can we forge against these enemies a grand and global alliance, North and South, East and West, that can assure a more fruitful life for all mankind? Will you join in that historic effort?

In the long history of the world, only a few generations have been granted the role of defending freedom in its hour of maximum danger. I do not shrink from this responsibility—I welcome it. I do not believe that any of us would exchange places with any other people or any other generation. The energy, the faith, the devotion which we bring to this endeavor will light our country and all who serve it. And the glow from that fire can truly light the world.

And so, my fellow Americans, ask not what your country can do for you; ask what you can do for your country.

My fellow citizens of the world, ask not what America will do for you, but what together we can do for the freedom of man.

Finally, whether you are citizens of America or citizens of the world, ask of us here the same high standards of strength and sacrifice which we ask of you. With a good conscience our only sure reward, with history the final judge of our deeds, let us go forth to lead the land we love, asking His blessing and His help, but knowing that here on earth God's work must truly be our own.

A great moment in Democratic history: Democratic President Harry S. Truman presides over the Potsdam Conference in July 1945 with Churchill and Stalin to decide what to do with the defeated Nazi Germany.

Trivia

1. Who is the founder of the Democratic Party?

2. Which president inspired the 22nd Amendment?

3. How many Democratic presidents died in office?

4. Who was the first black woman to run for the presidency?

5. What is the unofficial name of the Democratic Party?

6. Who was the only president to never marry?

7. Which Democratic vice presidents succeeded to the presidency?

8. Which president was the first to associate his Democratic campaign with the use of a cartoon donkey?

9. Who is the only president to win the Pulitzer Prize?

10. Who was the last incumbent Democratic president who decided to not seek reelection?

1. As a congressional caucus to fight for the Bill of Rights and against the Federalist Party, of which he was a member, Thomas Jefferson founded the Democratic Party in 1792 and ran under the ticket of Democrat-Republican and won in 1801.

2. Franklin Delano Roosevelt was elected to office four times. After FDR, the 22nd Amendment was ratified, which limits the presidential office to two terms.

3. Two. Franklin Delano Roosevelt and John F. Kennedy

4. In addition to being the first African-American woman elected to the U.S. Congress, Democrat Shirley Chisholm entered many presidential primaries in 1972 and received 151 delegate votes for the presidential nomination.

5. "The Party of the Common Man"

6. James Buchanan

7. Andrew Johnson became president after the assassination of Abraham Lincoln in 1865; Harry S. Truman assumed the presidency after Franklin D. Roosevelt died of a cerebral hemorrhage in 1945; Lyndon B. Johnson took over the presidency after John F. Kennedy was assassinated in 1963.

8. In response to his opponents calling him "a jackass," Democrat Andrew Jackson decided to turn the mudslinging on its head and use a symbol of a donkey in his campaign for the presidency in 1828.

9. John F. Kennedy, for his biography Profiles in Courage

10. Because internal polling showed that he was trailing in early primary states, Lyndon B. Johnson dropped out of the run for the presidency in 1968.

Children and Politics

I have been keenly interested in politics since I was a kid. It was impressed upon me at an early age by my grandfather that politics and voting were very important. As an adult, I wanted to pass this sense of civic duty on to my children.

During the 2004 election, my son was six and my daughter was eight. I decided that they were old enough to learn about the election process. I had taken them to the voting booth with me for every election since they were born. My daughter vaguely remembered the 2000 election, but my son didn't. I wanted to let them know how important voting is and that they needed to vote when they grew up.

I'm an extremely liberal Democrat. And I hope that my children will have the same political beliefs and values when they are adults. So I decided it was time to share those values with them. Of course, my friends claimed I was brainwashing them—but hey, they're my kids, and I can brainwash them if I want.

I took every opportunity to tell my children that Kerry was good and Bush was bad. They were still too young to understand the political platforms, so I just made it simple for them. Kerry is good. Bush is bad. At one point, my son even began mocking the president during speeches on TV. I could not have been a prouder mother.

On election day, we went to their school and waited our turn at the voting booth. They went with me, as always, and watched as I cast my ballot. I told them who I was voting for, and they were happy.

Later that night, we watched the votes come in on CNN. I explained the electoral college to them. We made it a game. Every state has a certain number of points. Whoever gets to 280 points wins. They were excited watching the states turn blue and red on the big map. I finally put them to bed, and they were disappointed that the election wasn't over yet. I told them they would find out about it in the morning.

I stayed up all night watching the election returns. And there still wasn't a result by morning. The kids got up for school and kept asking who won. I told them I didn't know yet, but that I would tell them as soon as I knew.

Kerry's concession came later in the afternoon. I was very disappointed. When my kids came home from school, I didn't say anything about the election. They went next door to their grandparents' house. I thought I'd just wait until later to give them the bad news.

My daughter walked back to the house after being at Grandma's for only about fifteen minutes. She looked so sad.

"What's wrong?" I asked.

"Kerry didn't win," she said, with tears in her eyes.

"I know," I said. And I hugged her.

A week later, we were having lunch at McDonald's. The TV in the restaurant was on CNN, and President Bush was speaking. My children saw the president, and their election frustration reared its ugly head.

"This is what I think of Bush," my son said, tearing his french fry to bits.

"Me, too," my daughter chimed in, squishing up her chicken nugget.

I smiled, but told them that they needed to eat and not destroy their food. But they kept going. Loudly. They kept saying "Bush stinks" over and over, followed by "Kerry's better." This went on for about a half-hour.

I started getting very weird looks from other restaurant patrons. I just knew that someone was going to say something about my children's political views. I tried to quiet them down. I told them that I agreed with them, but that other people might not. They didn't care. They were having fun. No one ever said anything, but they didn't have to. Their looks were enough.

Moral of the story? Children are capable of understanding politics and enjoying the process.

Second moral of the story? Taking politically minded children to public places after a disappointing election is a bad idea.

Lucy James

It was forty years ago this spring that Allard Lowenstein announced he was running for Congress from my district on Long Island. Lowenstein, the architect of the dump-Johnson movement and the man behind Eugene McCarthy's antiwar presidential candidacy, was dubbed the Pied Piper. His campaign attracted young, smart, liberal students who gave up their weekends or more to be part of his campaign. Lowenstein's cadre of young volunteers included Barney Frank, Gary Hart, and me.

Nineteen sixty-eight was a tumultuous year. The Vietnam War raged on. The Tet offensive left us reeling. Then Martin Luther King was assassinated. Campuses all over the world erupted, and police reacted with extreme force. The world was a mess.

I was a mess, too. I was starting high school. I'd outgrown my friends—girls who had sleepover dates in pink pajamas and fuzzy slippers and thumbed through the pages of *Tiger Beat* magazine. When the alpha girls invited me to the mall, I found no joy in shopping for earrings and miniskirts.

The older brother of one of my friends from camp was drafted. While classmates were watching episodes of *Dark Shadows*, I was tracking the war dead, my outrage growing. I tried to channel my fury into antiwar speeches on the debate team, and wrote melancholy poems for the high school literary magazine. I couldn't find where I fit in and wasn't sure, given the state of the world, that I wanted to.

I couldn't vote. I didn't have a license, but I had something that proved to be more valuable—my mother's permission.

My mother, whose politics had always leaned left, had taken me to an antiwar rally where Al Lowenstein spoke. He was a tall man in a hopelessly wrinkled suit and thick black glasses, and looked more like a grocer than a leader. But he was speaking out eloquently against the Vietnam War. He said that one by one we could change the world by standing up for what we believed. Lowenstein recounted the successful voter registration drives he'd orchestrated in the South. Like everyone else in that low-ceilinged basement room in the local synagogue, I began to believe that we could stop the war. In that spring without hope, Lowenstein's message was welcome. He pledged to us, "When you see injustice, you have to stand up, and I will stand up. I will stand up for you if you elect me."

I pledged my allegiance to Lowenstein. When I told my parents I wanted to work on his campaign, they heartily approved. I spent all my nonschool waking hours at Lowenstein's storefront headquarters, coming home late at night smelling like fried chicken from the Chicken Delight restaurant next store. We used the storefront location, by the Long Island Rail Road station, to our advantage. We put on our biggest smiles and handed homebound commuters campaign literature, or fortune cookies that said inside, "Vote Al Lowenstein for Change."

As one of the youngest volunteers, my main task was stuffing envelopes, which I did with enthusiasm deep into the night, past my previous bedtime, using the rubber stamp that said "Friends of Al Lowenstein Committee" for the return address. When I finally got home, I'd fall asleep dreaming of the red ink and broken serif type of the stamp pad . . . and of Billy.

Billy was my age, had the beginnings of a scruffy beard, and eyes that turned the color of cucumber when he was making a point. He was articulate enough to debate with the college kids. He thought I was smart and funny, and I'd never met anyone like him.

A couple of weeks before the June Democratic primary, I was teamed up with Billy for weekend canvassing at the Green Acres Mall. It was a big shopping weekend and a great opportunity for Al to talk to the voters. When the weather forecast was revised the night before the event, one of the volunteer coordinators thought we would need more flyers to cover increased mall traffic.

Suddenly I had a useful skill to offer: I could type and, from the literary magazine, I knew how to work a mimeograph machine. I retyped the flyer text onto the stencil, careful to hit the keys evenly, but the o's and b's looked like black blobs. I yanked the paper out of the manual typewriter. The roller made a trill-like sound, kind of like my Spanish teacher when she was angry. I found a bottle of Obliter-ine, dipped the small brush into the purple liquid, and covered the errant marks. The sharp-smelling correction fluid made me cry as I turned the hand crank hard and fast, producing my flyers.

Billy and I were told to concentrate on talking to mothers with the message that Al was against sending their sons to war. As the youngest volunteers, it would be most effective coming from us. The college students would engage in conversation on other issues. It was my first lesson in marketing.

Billy and I drew people over, cracking jokes, carrying their pack-ages (and stuffing my flyer into their bags)—anything to get them to meet Al. Lowenstein ducked his handlers and stayed in the area manned by Billy and me. He made us feel like we were the only two people in the world, like we could make a difference.

Billy and I had to walk home after the event. We crossed over Sunrise Highway, which neither of us was allowed to do, and sat by the duck pond. It was a cheerless afternoon, and I envied the ducks who were still wearing their winter fat. I had a copy of the flyer folded into the small pocket of my Landlubbers. Billy had a half-eaten bagel. We fed the ducks. Then we kissed.

It wasn't my first kiss—I wasn't quite that young—but it was the first one that really mattered. It was 1968, and swirling amid the turmoil there was promise.

Stephanie Feuer

From the Lips of Children

The year was 1996. We said good-bye to Barbara Jordan, Gene Kelly, and George Burns. We heard, not understanding or quite believing it, of the first successful clone: Dolly the Sheep. Politically, we would choose between returning President Clinton to office or replacing him with Bob Dole. My hometown hockey team, the Colorado Avalanche, swept the Stanley Cup finals and brought Denver its first major championship.

None of that meant a lot to me. I was a single mom trying to make ends meet, dealing with a troubled teenage son and a bright but mentally ill daughter. Writing and church activities provided pinpoints of light in the drudgery of my life.

When the music director offered me the privilege of writing a short musical for the fourth of July, I developed a simple concept. I would tie the concerns and prayers of Americans during previous presidential elections with patriotic songs.

In 1792, America chose our first president and prayed for the grand experiment of democracy to succeed. The choir sang "My Country, 'Tis of Thee." In 1860, the country divided over slavery and the threat of war. The song: "Mine Eyes Have Seen the Glory." In 1932, depression held the economy in a firm grip. The natural choice was "God Bless America."

I wanted something special for the last section—a prayer for the current election. So I turned to my favorite people: the children I taught in Sunday school, ranging in age from five to twelve.

Our congregation was tiny, white, conservative (read: "Republican," myself being a rare exception), and was weighted toward older members. The size of the children's classes varied from one to eight. On the Sunday we wrote the prayer for the current election, four children were present. Two sisters huddled side by side, the kindergartener clinging to her older sister like a leech. An eight-year-old boy, a bit of a problem student, bounced in and out of chairs. My daughter, the senior statesman at twelve, was easily the most articulate.

From this unlikely group came this powerful prayer:

We pray for our Earth:
    For wildlife to be protected.
    For the national parks to stay open.
    For people to recycle and not cut down trees.
    For people to care for the Earth.
We pray for our nation:
    For both the budget and taxes to go down.
    For all children to get a good education, no matter where they live.
We pray for our people:
    For the homeless.
    For people, especially children, who need health care.
    For our children. Don't let them live in violence.
We ask that the right man be elected president in November.

I didn't have to teach my class anything about democracy. They already understood what was important.

Darlene Franklin

The Only Living Democrat in Brooklyn

I don't live in what you'd call a neighborhood rich in Democrats.

As a matter of fact, my neighborhood isn't one for local color at all—pretty much everyone dresses in black and white. You'd recognize it from movies, TV cop shows (usually with an undercover detective trying to blend in, always unsuccessfully), and even *The Simpsons:* this is the Hasidic part of Brooklyn, New York.

Here, people look at politics like a football game, or like a very intense and long-running game of Scrabble. I couldn't tell you why exactly—it might be that we're so removed from the rest of the world, or it might be that we put our faith in God to control things more than some guy in a starched shirt and a tie the color of the flag. We talk about politics with a mixture of distance (like it won't affect us) and rabid fascination (like driving by a car crash)—we don't care, but we can't tear our eyes away from it.

At Friday night Sabbath dinners, everyone's joking about Obama. The matter under discussion is an e-mail forward accusing the presidential candidate of being affiliated with a radical faction of militant Muslims. I immediately recognize the e-mail in question—it's the one that has been disavowed and disproved by all sane and right-minded people and by virtually every politician in the race. Even Hillary, who at this point wouldn't let

Barack Obama get away with saying that he brushes his teeth every morning without trying to disprove it, has admitted this e-mail is malicious, offensive, and untrue. For crying out loud—how do my fellow dining companions still believe it's true?

Unwisely, my mouth opens. Even more unwisely, I try to point this out to them. "That's ridiculous," I say. "For one thing, Obama is Christian. For another—"

"Of course it's true," the host of the evening says. "I saw the photos in the paper. This man, Osama, he was wearing a Muslim dress."

AAAAHHH!!! Who *else* in the world still makes Obama/Osama jokes? Even worse, who makes that mistake *honestly*?

I suppose I shouldn't talk. I didn't grow up this way. I became Orthodox about ten years ago, and I'm still learning how to be that way. I've learned a lot. Sometimes I completely surprise myself by thinking in Hebrew. Other times, I can't understand what I'm thinking, and I wind up with a massive headache.

I'm never afraid of speaking my mind. It's not always a good thing, but it can be. Like that night at dinner, when I talked about how the abuse that Obama's getting is the same abuse that Jews have been getting for thousands of years—especially people who look Jewish, with black hats and overcoats and big bushy beards.

I once got attacked on the street in San Francisco for wearing a yarmulke, when a bunch of people supposedly on the way to a Middle East peace march picked a fight with my friend and me, stopping us on the street and calling us Arab-killers and racists. No one's immune from racism, just like no one's immune from being a racist.

After I spoke up, my friends looked at things a little differently, I think. They might not be waiting outside the polls with stacks of Obama flyers in their hands, but I think their minds opened up a little bit that night.

And, living here, my mind's opened up a bit, too. The Torah teaches that at least 10 percent of our income and 10 percent of our time should be donated to charity, and nowhere is that more commonly practiced than among Hasidic Jews. When a family in the community goes hungry, or even if they just don't have enough money for a nice Sabbath meal, people join together and take care of them. And this symbiosis isn't only among a few families, or a few hundred. When I say "the community," I'm talking in the thousands.

It's not just neighbors, either, or just Jews. I always called myself an environmentalist because I gave five bucks to Greenpeace twice a year. My community taught me that for every eight-hour day I work, one hour should be for someone else and not me.

More than that, they taught me about the power of speech. Yeah, I taught them a few things. But, after I ranted a bit about unemployment and homelessness and Republican indifference, an old rabbi at the table said that we had to be careful of our words because we are what our words proclaim us to be. "If you see other people and they seem obnoxious, it's because you're obnoxious on the inside. If you look at them and you think you're ugly, then, *gevalt,* the truth is, you're ugly. But if you look at them and see holiness—then, *mamish,* you're a holy person."

The last thing I remember about that night before walking home, stuffed full and drunk on sweet, yellow raisin bread and other amazing food, was staring at the rabbi, widening my eyes, and trying to focus on him with my entire range of vision—trying to see, to the exclusion of everything else in the world, holiness.

Matthue Roth

A Tried-and-True View of Everything Blue

WHO SAID IT?

"If we have no sense of community, the American dream will wither."

—*William Clinton*

"Office holders are the agents of the people, not their masters."

—*Grover Cleveland*

"All free governments are managed by the combined wisdom and folly of the people."

—*James Garfield*

"We must adjust to changing times and still hold to unchanging principles."

—*Jimmy Carter*

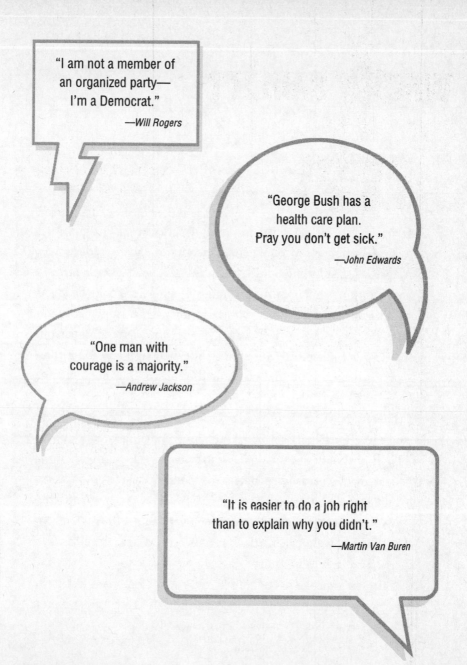

"I am not a member of an organized party—I'm a Democrat."
—*Will Rogers*

"George Bush has a health care plan. Pray you don't get sick."
—*John Edwards*

"One man with courage is a majority."
—*Andrew Jackson*

"It is easier to do a job right than to explain why you didn't."
—*Martin Van Buren*

Lyndon B. Johnson
"We Shall Overcome"
Delivered March 15, 1965

I speak tonight for the dignity of man and the destiny of democracy. I urge every member of both parties, Americans of all religions and of all colors, from every section of this country, to join me in that cause.

At times, history and fate meet at a single time in a single place to shape a turning point in man's unending search for freedom. So it was at Lexington and Concord. So it was a century ago at Appomattox. So it was last week in Selma, Alabama. There, long-suffering men and women peacefully protested the denial of their rights as Americans. Many of them were brutally assaulted. One good man—a man of God—was killed.

There is no cause for pride in what has happened in Selma. There is no cause for self-satisfaction in the long denial of equal rights of millions of Americans. But there is cause for hope and for faith in our democracy in what is happening here tonight. For the cries of pain and the hymns and protests of oppressed people have summoned into convocation all the majesty of this great government—the government of the greatest nation on Earth. Our mission is at once the oldest and the most basic of this country—to right wrong, to do justice, to serve man. In our time we have come to live with the moments of great crises. Our lives have been marked with debate about great issues, issues of war and peace, issues of prosperity and depression.

But rarely in any time does an issue lay bare the secret heart of America itself. Rarely are we met with a challenge, not to our growth or abundance, or our welfare or our security, but rather to the values and the purposes and the meaning of our beloved nation. The issue of equal rights for American Negroes is such an issue. And should we defeat every enemy, and should we double our wealth and conquer the stars, and still be unequal to this issue, then we will have failed as a people and as a nation. For, with a country as with a person, "what is a man profited if he shall gain the whole world, and lose his own soul?"

There is no Negro problem. There is no southern problem. There is no northern problem. There is only an American problem.

And we are met here tonight as Americans—not as Democrats or Republicans; we're met here as Americans to solve that problem. This was the first nation in the history of the world to be founded with a purpose.

The great phrases of that purpose still sound in every American heart, North and South: "All men are created equal." "Government by consent of the governed." "Give me liberty or give me death." And those are not just clever words, and those are not just empty theories. In their name Americans have fought and died for two centuries, and tonight around the world they stand there as guardians of our liberty risking their lives. Those words are promised to every citizen that he shall share in the dignity of man. This dignity cannot be found in a man's possessions. It cannot be found in his power or in his position. It really rests on his right to be treated as a man equal in opportunity to all others. It says that he shall share in freedom. He shall choose his leaders, educate his children, provide for his family according to his ability and his merits as a human being.

To apply any other test, to deny a man his hopes because of his color or race or his religion or the place of his birth is not only to do injustice, it is to deny Americans and to dishonor the dead who gave their lives for American freedom. Our fathers believed that if this noble view of the rights of man was to flourish it must be rooted in democracy. This most basic right of all was the right to choose your own leaders. The history of this country in large measure is the history of expansion of the right to all of our people.

Many of the issues of civil rights are very complex and most difficult. But about this there can and should be no argument: every American citizen must have an equal right to vote. There is no reason which can excuse the denial of that right. There is no duty which weighs more heavily on us than the duty we have to insure that right. Yet the harsh fact is that in many places in this country men and women are kept from voting simply because they are Negroes.

Every device of which human ingenuity is capable has been used to deny this right. The Negro citizen may go to register only to be told that the day is wrong, or the hour is late, or the official in charge is absent. And if he persists, and if he manages to present himself to the registrar, he may be disqualified because he did not spell out his middle name, or because he abbreviated a word on the application. And if he manages to fill out an application, he is given a test. The registrar is the sole judge of whether he passes this test. He may be asked to recite the entire Constitution, or explain the most complex provisions of state law.

And even a college degree cannot be used to prove that he can read and write. For the fact is that the only way to pass these barriers is to show a white skin. Experience has clearly shown that the existing process of law cannot overcome systematic and ingenious discrimination. No law that we now have on the books, and I have helped to put three of them there, can insure the right to vote when local officials are determined to deny it. In such a case, our duty must be clear to all of us. The Constitution says that no person shall be kept from voting because of his race or his color.

We have all sworn an oath before God to support and to defend that Constitution. We must now act in obedience to that oath. Wednesday, I will send to Congress a law designed to eliminate illegal barriers to the right to vote. The broad principles of that bill will be in the hands of the Democratic and Republican leaders tomorrow. After they have reviewed it, it will come here formally as a bill. I am grateful for this opportunity to come here tonight at the invitation of the leadership to reason with my friends, to give them my views, and to visit with my former colleagues.

I have had prepared a more comprehensive analysis of the legislation which I had intended to transmit to the clerk tomorrow, but which I will submit to the clerks tonight. But I want to really discuss the main proposals of this legislation. This bill will strike down restrictions to voting in all elections, federal, state and local, which have been used to deny Negroes the right to vote.

This bill will establish a simple, uniform standard which cannot be used, however ingenious the effort, to flout our Constitution. It will provide for citizens to be registered by officials of the United States Government, if the state officials refuse to register them. It will eliminate tedious, unnecessary lawsuits which delay the right to vote. Finally, this legislation will insure that properly registered individuals are not prohibited from voting. I will welcome the suggestions from all the members of Congress—I have no doubt that I will get some—on ways and means to strengthen this law and to make it effective.

But experience has plainly shown that this is the only path to carry out the command of the Constitution. To those who seek to avoid action by their national government in their home communities, who want to and who seek to maintain purely local control over elections, the answer is simple: open your polling places to all your people. Allow men and women to register and vote whatever the color of their skin. Extend the rights of citizenship to every citizen of this land. There is no Constitutional issue here. The command of the Constitution is plain. There is no moral issue. It is wrong—deadly wrong—to deny any of your fellow Americans the right to vote in this country.

There is no issue of state's rights or national rights. There is only the struggle for human rights. I have not the slightest doubt what will be your answer. But the last time a President sent a civil rights bill to the Congress it contained a provision to protect voting rights in Federal elections. That civil rights bill was passed after eight long months of debate. And when that bill came to my desk from the Congress for signature, the heart of the voting provision had been eliminated.

This time, on this issue, there must be no delay, or no hesitation, or no compromise with our purpose. We cannot, we must not, refuse to protect the right of every American to vote in every election that he may desire to participate in.

And we ought not, and we cannot, and we must not wait another eight months before we get a bill. We have already waited 100 years and more, and the time for waiting is gone. So I ask you to join me in working long hours and nights and weekends, if necessary, to pass this bill. And I don't make that request lightly, for, from the window where I sit, with the problems of our country, I recognize that from outside this chamber is the outraged conscience of a nation, the grave concern of many nations, and the harsh judgment of history on our acts.

But even if we pass this bill the battle will not be over. What happened in Selma is part of a far larger movement which reaches into every section and state of America. It is the effort of American Negroes to secure for themselves the full blessings of American life. Their cause must be our cause too. Because it's not just Negroes, but really it's all of us, who must overcome the crippling legacy of bigotry and injustice.

And we shall overcome.

As a man whose roots go deeply into southern soil, I know how agonizing racial feelings are. I know how difficult it is to reshape the attitudes and the structure of our society. But a century has passed—more than 100 years—since the Negro was freed. And he is not fully free tonight. It was more than 100 years ago that Abraham Lincoln—a great President of another party—signed the Emancipation Proclamation. But emancipation is a proclamation and not a fact.

A century has passed—more than 100 years—since equality was promised, and yet the Negro is not equal. A century has passed since the day of promise, and the promise is unkept. The time of justice has now come, and I tell you that I believe sincerely that no force can hold it back. It is right in the eyes of man and God that it should come, and when it does, I think that day will brighten the lives of every American. For Negroes are not the only victims. How many white children have gone uneducated? How many white families have lived in stark poverty? How many white lives have been scarred by fear, because we wasted energy and our substance to maintain the barriers of hatred and terror?

And so I say to all of you here and to all in the nation tonight that those who appeal to you to hold on to the past do so at the cost of denying you your future. This great, rich, restless country can offer opportunity and education and hope to all—all, black and white, North and South, sharecropper and city dweller. These are the enemies: poverty, ignorance, disease. They are our enemies, not our fellow man, not our neighbor.

And these enemies, too—poverty, disease, and ignorance—we shall overcome.

Now let none of us in any section look with prideful righteousness on the troubles in another section or the problems of our neighbors. There is really no part of America where the promise of equality has been fully kept. In Buffalo as well as in Birmingham, in Philadelphia as well as Selma, Americans are struggling for the fruits of freedom.

This is one nation. What happens in Selma and Cincinnati is a matter of legitimate concern to every American. But let each of us look within our own hearts and our own communities, and let each of us put our shoulder to the wheel to root out injustice wherever it exists. As we meet here in this peaceful historic chamber tonight, men from the South, some of whom were at Iwo Jima, men from the North who have carried Old Glory to the far corners of the world and who brought it back without a stain on it, men from the East and from the West are all fighting together without regard to religion or color or region in Vietnam.

Men from every region fought for us across the world twenty years ago. And now in these common dangers, in these common sacrifices, the South made its contribution of honor and gallantry no less than any other region in the great republic.

And in some instances, a great many of them, more. And I have not the slightest doubt that good men from everywhere in this country, from the Great Lakes to the Gulf of Mexico, from the Golden Gate to the harbors along the Atlantic, will rally now together in this cause to vindicate the freedom of all Americans. For all of us owe this duty, and I believe that all of us will respond to it.

Your President makes that request of every American.

The real hero of this struggle is the American Negro. His actions and protests, his courage to risk safety, and even to risk his life, have awakened the conscience of this nation. His demonstrations have been designed to call attention to injustice, designed to provoke change, designed to stir reform. He has been called upon to make good the promise of America.

And who among us can say that we would have made the same progress were it not for his persistent bravery and his faith in American democracy? For at the real heart of the battle for equality is a deep-seated belief in the democratic process. Equality depends, not on the force of arms or tear gas, but depends upon the force of moral right—not on recourse to violence, but on respect for law and order.

There have been many pressures upon your President, and there will be others as the days come and go. But I pledge to you tonight that we intend to fight this battle where it should be fought—in the courts, and in the Congress, and the hearts of men. We must preserve the right of free speech and the right of free assembly. But the right of free speech does not carry with it—as has been said—the right to holler fire in a crowded theater.

We must preserve the right to free assembly. But free assembly does not carry with it the right to block public thoroughfares to traffic. We do have a right to protest. And a right to march under conditions that do not infringe the Constitutional rights of our neighbors. And I intend to protect all those rights as long as I am permitted to serve in this office.

We will guard against violence, knowing it strikes from our hands the very weapons which we seek—progress, obedience to law, and belief in American values. In Selma, as elsewhere, we seek and pray for peace. We seek order, we seek unity, but we will not accept the peace of stifled rights or the order imposed by fear, or the unity that stifles protest—for peace cannot be purchased at the cost of liberty.

In Selma tonight—and we had a good day there—as in every city we are working for a just and peaceful settlement. We must all remember after this speech I'm making tonight, after the police and the F.B.I.

and the Marshals have all gone, and after you have promptly passed this bill, the people of Selma and the other cities of the nation must still live and work together.

And when the attention of the nation has gone elsewhere, they must try to heal the wounds and to build a new community. This cannot be easily done on a battleground of violence as the history of the South itself shows. It is in recognition of this that men of both races have shown such an outstandingly impressive responsibility in recent days— last Tuesday and again today.

The bill I am presenting to you will be known as a civil rights bill. But in a larger sense, most of the program I am recommending is a civil rights program. Its object is to open the city of hope to all people of all races, because all Americans just must have the right to vote, and we are going to give them that right.

All Americans must have the privileges of citizenship, regardless of race, and they are going to have those privileges of citizenship regardless of race.

But I would like to caution you and remind you that to exercise these privileges takes much more than just legal rights. It requires a trained mind and a healthy body. It requires a decent home and the chance to find a job and the opportunity to escape from the clutches of poverty.

Of course, people cannot contribute to the nation if they are never taught to read or write; if their bodies are stunted from hunger; if their sickness goes untended; if their life is spent in hopeless poverty, just drawing a welfare check.

So we want to open the gates to opportunity. But we're also going to give all our people, black and white, the help that they need to walk through those gates. My first job after college was as a teacher in Cotulla, Texas, in a small Mexican-American school. Few of them could speak English, and I couldn't speak much Spanish. My students were poor, and they often came to class without breakfast and hungry. And they knew even in their youth the pain of prejudice. They never seemed to know why people disliked them, but they knew it was so because I saw it in their eyes.

I often walked home late in the afternoon after the classes were finished wishing there was more that I could do. But all I knew was to teach them the little that I knew, hoping that I might help them against the hardships that lay ahead. And somehow you never forget what poverty and hatred can do when you see its scars on the hopeful face of a young child.

I never thought then, in 1928, that I would be standing here in 1965. It never even occurred to me in my fondest dreams that I might have the chance to help the sons and daughters of those students, and to help people like them all over this country. But now I do have that chance.

And I'll let you in on a secret—I mean to use it. And I hope that you will use it with me.

This is the richest, most powerful country which ever occupied this globe. The might of past empires is little compared to ours. But I do not want to be the President who built empires, or sought grandeur, or extended dominion.

I want to be the President who educated young children to the wonders of their world. I want to be the President who helped to feed the hungry and to prepare them to be taxpayers instead of tax eaters. I want to be the President who helped the poor to find their own way and who protected the right of every citizen to vote in every election. I want to be the President who helped to end hatred among his fellow men and who promoted love among the people of all races, all regions, and all parties. I want to be the President who helped to end war among the brothers of this Earth.

And so, at the request of your beloved Speaker and the Senator from Montana, the Majority Leader, the Senator from Illinois, the Minority Leader, Mr. McCullock and other members of both parties, I came here tonight, not as President Roosevelt came down one time in person to veto a bonus bill; not as President Truman came down one time to urge passage of a railroad bill, but I came down here to ask you to share this task with me. And to share it with the people that we both work for.

I want this to be the Congress—Republicans and Democrats alike—which did all these things for all these people. Beyond this great chamber—out yonder—in fifty states are the people that we serve. Who can tell what deep and unspoken hopes are in their hearts tonight as they sit there and listen? We all can guess, from our own lives, how difficult they often find their own pursuit of happiness, how many problems each little family has. They look most of all to themselves for their future, but I think that they also look to each of us.

Above the pyramid on the Great Seal of the United States it says in Latin, "God has favored our undertaking." God will not favor everything that we do. It is rather our duty to divine His will. But I cannot help but believe that He truly understands and that He really favors the undertaking that we begin here tonight.

A great moment in Democratic history: Moments after taking the presidential oath of office, John Fitzgerald Kennedy implores Americans to "ask not what your country can do for you, ask what you can do for your country."

1. What was the origin of Tammany Hall?

2. Who is the longest serving member of the Senate?

3. Who is the first woman to serve as Speaker of the House?

4. Who was the first Jewish candidate for vice president?

5. Which Democratic presidents won a Nobel Peace Prize?

6. How were Democratic presidential candidates selected before the creation of national conventions?

7. Who was the first woman to serve as a senator?

8. What vice president was indicted for murder while in office and later tried for treason?

9. Who is the only Democratic vice president to win the Nobel Peace Prize?

10. What president saw two vice presidents die during his term of office?

1. The Tammany Society was founded on May 12, 1789, as a fraternal organization. Aaron Burr transformed the Society into a political force that supported the Democratic-Republican ticket in 1800. In 1830, the Society moved into its own building, and from that time on was known as Tammany Hall.

2. Senator Robert C. Byrd of West Virginia, who has been in office since January 3, 1959. As a member of the House and Senate, Byrd is second in service only to Carl Hayden of Arizona, who spent fifty-six years in Congress. Byrd may soon surpass that record.

3. Nancy Pelosi of California, Speaker since 2007

4. Senator Joseph Lieberman of Connecticut in 2000

5. Woodrow Wilson in 1919 and Jimmy Carter in 2002

6. James Madison and James Monroe were nominated by Congressional Caucuses.

7. Rebecca Latimer Felton of Georgia was appointed to fill an unexpired term, and served one day, November 21–22, 1922 before the newly elected senator took office. At eighty-seven, Felton was the oldest freshman to enter the Senate.

8. Aaron Burr, vice president 1801–1805. He was indicted for killing Alexander Hamilton in an 1804 duel and tried for a conspiracy to invade Spanish territory from the United States.

9. Albert A. Gore, Jr. in 2007. Two Republican vice presidents won the Nobel Peace Prize, Theodore Roosevelt in 1906 and Charles Dawes in 1925.

10. James Madison. Both his vice presidents died in office, George Clinton 1809–1812, and Elbridge Gerry 1813–1814.

It Takes a Transatlantic Passage

Marriage to a hard-core Republican, while I balanced on the opposite end of the fulcrum, was not exactly what I had in mind the second time around. I recognized our differences within an hour of meeting my future husband, Bob, at the Hoar House. Even the name of the historically designated restaurant and lounge should have given me some pause to reconsider. Over a glass of wine that evening and several arguments later—the cost of insurance versus universal health care, National Public Radio versus conservative talk radio stations—I was in love. Was I crazy? Even food differences were notable: one of us relished the sweetness of beef tartar and oysters on the half shell, while the other lusted for fresh vegetables, whole-grain bread, and fruit.

Marriage led to debates over President Bush's war in Iraq versus President Clinton's wandering ways. Neither of us could comprehend the other's perspectives on politics.

Conversations at the dinner table unfolded like this:

"How could you vote for Kerry?"

"How could you vote for G. W.?"

"Are you trying to pick a fight?"

"Here we go again. So how's the weather?"

"How did you *ever* connect?" we're asked. A good question. Opposites attract, I suggest. Variety is the spice of life, perhaps.

The reality, however, is that we bonded on a sailboat. We retired early and made a transatlantic passage on our forty-two-foot sloop, *Conestoga*. We depended upon each other for survival. The challenges involved boat maintenance and care, our physical well-being and safety, and remaining aboard. Bob posted a sign in the head (or bathroom): "Do not leave the ship without the captain's permission!" We wanted to live to tell our story.

It was the two of us alone on our boat, each taking watches, each staying alert during storms as the seas roared and waves crashed on the deck. When a line parted so that we could not raise our mainsail, I shakily cranked Bob up to the top of the mast in a bosun's seat. In rolling seas, he cut the line. Trust and respect grew.

It was three heads—his, mine, and the Spanish-speaking mechanic—that hovered over a malfunctioning engine in a small Spanish port while trying to communicate with only a Spanish-English dictionary. Solving engine problems became a greater concern than American political life. Staying afloat was essential. Life mattered.

This was the gift of our sailing adventure to the Mediterranean Sea. Yes, it was an opportunity to explore fascinating cultures and meet interesting people. But, ultimately, the voyage was about us and our relationship with each other. We became pals and depended on each other. We divided chores; each of us participated fully. My hearing was better; his eyes were stronger. At sea, he was the captain. On land, I often claimed the distinction. And as we journeyed and overcame obstacles together, we forgave each other for our imperfections, even political ones.

Now our conversations at dinner unfold like this:

"How could you vote for Hillary?"

"How could you support McCain?"

"Here we go again. I love you."

"I love you, too!"

Our human differences have taken on a different perspective. Loving kindness is more important than political debates. Being happy is more noteworthy than being right. So, I join land trusts and literary circles. He saves his political conversations for men's groups and business associates in this Republican community. And we're still married—for eighteen years.

Elizabeth Phillips-Hershey, Ph.D.

The Donkey Club: Memories of a Precinct Captain's Daughter

My father was not a man of immense wealth, business acumen, or scholarly ability. Thank goodness a man's greatness need not be measured by these standards. He was a man of modest but comfortable means. He was a sincere, loyal, and charitable human being who had the utmost regard for people, irrespective of race, color, or creed. Dad was everyone's friend, and he was the neighborhood "Democratic precinct captain."

My perceptions of the "precinct captain" are based upon my recollections as a child growing up in Chicago. Politics was a part of my life. Our apartment was home to my parents, two younger sisters, and my grandmother. In this home filled with three generations of family and mass confusion, I thrived.

My dad, Charles (nicknamed Chuck), was muscular, about 5 feet, 8 inches tall, and had a smile that could melt the coldest of hearts. He was a loyal Democrat who took his position and the responsibility it encompassed seriously because politics was his love.

I remember how my father would awaken full of energy and exhilaration the morning of an election day. He'd leave home before dawn and arrive home twenty-four hours later, with his polling sheet in hand, boasting with pride of the votes he'd delivered for the Democratic candidates of that particular election year.

The precinct captain, as I knew him, helped people. Often he was the spokesman for his neighbors and would request favors on their behalf.

I remember one evening when the family was watching the new "magic screen," and the bell rang at seven o'clock. It was Rosa, a young woman with two small children. She was an alcoholic and periodically visited the precinct captain. Rosa was hysterical because she had squandered her money on alcohol and had no money to feed her children. Often my father handed her a few dollars. This particular night, after a brief discussion with my mother, he refused Rosa's request. Instead he escorted her to the corner grocery store.

Dad was gone a long time. My sisters and I sat in the kitchen with my mother as we anxiously awaited his return.

"Chuck, where were you so long?" asked my mother when my dad returned.

"I took Rosa shopping for food. This way I'll know the babies will have enough to eat until her check arrives."

Dad turned to us. "Remember, if you have a loaf of bread, eggs, milk, and butter, you'll never go hungry."

Till this day, my refrigerator is always filled with the "necessities." They represent love, kindness, and a full belly.

In the early fifties, Democratic political strongholds were branching out, and Chicago's Democratic precinct captains found they were losing touch with one another. Thus in 1954 they founded a club to keep their group together. Since the donkey is the symbol of the Democratic Party, they called their club the Donkey Club. My father was one of its founders.

The fundamental principles and purposes of the Donkey Club were to bring together Democratic precinct captains and their assistants to work for the success of Chicago's Democratic organization. Their ideals and purposes were to work collectively for the equality of all people, regardless of race, color, or creed.

The club was also a social club where the men could come together for an evening of relaxation as they discussed politics. My dad's devotion was unyielding.

Campaigning now took on a new meaning. The entire family took to the shopping malls. We handed out stickers, buttons, and campaign information. When a candidate was elected, the captains collectively received recognition. This was important to the club. With the addition of each new prominent political figure, the club gained increased recognition.

After having served several terms as treasurer, Dad was elected president of the Donkey Club. He worked diligently. His dedication to the club was expressed in the following excerpt from his acceptance speech.

> *I have, since the inception of the Donkey Club, worked hard and long to make this club and all that it stands for a success. I sincerely believe that as an integral part of Chicago's Democratic organization, it serves a vital and useful purpose. Each of us has a duty and obligation to devote our time and efforts to benefit our community.*

Before a major election, the club held a dinner dance. The ballroom of one hotel or another was filled with well-dressed men and women. My father, as president, reigned majestic in his black tuxedo, while my mother, beautifully attired, stood by his side. They reigned as regally as any "First Couple."

As the room filled with family, friends, and supporters of the organization, my sisters and I anxiously awaited the arrival of the dignitaries who had been invited. Their appearance gave credence to the club. Dad would stand before the rostrum beaming as he introduced with both pride and humility dignitaries such as Mayor Richard Daley, Adlai Stevenson, and Jack Kennedy.

When a Democratic candidate won, my family celebrated. When a candidate lost, we shared Dad's sorrow.

My father believed in the two-party system. He was a patriotic man who worried about his government and his country. In an era when the word *politics* sometimes brought a snicker to the lips of many, my dad was a "good guy." He had no power, no campaign funds, and very little clout. He was a man who never comprised his principles. His name was never on a Democratic ballot, and the highest offices he ever held, besides president of the Donkey Club, were husband and father. He was your old-time precinct captain—who knew his people by first name and considered all of them his friends. When he died many years ago, they all came to his funeral—hundreds of his "friends." He would have loved that had he known, because above all he valued friendship.

Myrna Beth Lambert

A Marriage of Politics

My conservative Republican in-laws thought it was hysterically funny when I, as a new bride, told them I grew up in a town with only one Republican. Time and again, I heard them sharing this knowledge with friends and other family members, and for the first few years they found this cute. There was lots of laughter.

As far as I know, I was telling the truth. I grew up in a small Florida town and knew only one Republican. She was an attractive, courteous woman who always spoke to me and had a ready smile. Little did she know that I never saw her without thinking, *She's a Republican*. I paid close attention to her dress, which was much like the other women in town; to her manners, which were Southern to the core; and to her general bearing. *What made her a Republican?* I wondered. *What was there about her that I couldn't see?* To my young mind, the very word "Republican" seemed not only negative, but tinged with an unpleasantness I couldn't name.

The early years of my marriage were spent in Michigan, but eventually my husband honored an earlier promise to me. When he finished graduate school, he took me back home to Florida. I hadn't grown up singing "I'll Take You Home Again, Kathleen" without learning something.

With a full-time job, warm climate, and steady paycheck, we were in a position not only to eat better, but to consider the wider world around us. Our first priorities were to get library cards and register to vote.

What evil pleasure it gave me when I wrote my in-laws to let them know my young husband was now a registered Democrat! Evil pleasure it was. My father-in-law sent a blistering letter by return mail. After all, *his* father had fought for the Union in the Civil War—under Sherman, no less. At seventeen he had stood on tiptoe to be accepted into the army, only to be disgraced by his youngest grandson's wife all these years later.

It was more than three months before my father-in-law spoke to me again. That's how important politics was in this family, never mind that I had broken tradition by marrying a Yankee (though by now this Yankee had learned not to use the expression, "Like Grant took Richmond").

My father-in-law never broached the matter with us again, but there was good-natured ribbing among my husband's brothers and sisters each time a presidential election rolled around. We were good citizens, and if we were to be out of town during an election, we secured absentee ballots. After one of our candidates won, my sister-in-law informed us that in a landslide victory, they didn't count the absentee ballots. It was all good-natured. Then.

Did politics change or did our natures change as we matured? I boasted once that I voted for the man. And I did, once. Then in the '70s the very word "Republican" began to take on a nasty edge once more. I saw a chink in the armor of our great country, a chink in the armor of the "R" in Republican. Exchanges with my brothers and sisters-in-law took on a sharper tone than in recent years. More time passed, and I noticed a change in the two parties. Were the policies of Republicans and Democrats, like some aging couple, melding, becoming more alike? Did we still have a two-party system?

In 2008, the presidential primaries are upon us. In some ways, Republicans and Democrats may be joined at the hip, but given the level of people's dissatisfaction over pressing concerns—global warming, rumors of yet more wars, recession, inflation, impeachment, torture, and illegal aliens—sore issues aren't scabbing over.

E-mails fly back and forth between our families, and they are often laced with the unhappiness and disagreements of politics. Even my husband and I have disagreed. As a child I can recall my mother telling my dad she was going to kill his vote. He looked grim, as though questioning the wisdom of having given women the right to vote in the first place. I thought it was funny until last week when I heard myself saying the same thing to my husband. He came to me the next evening and asked that we agree on a candidate. No killing votes. No harsh words. We agreed, and I'm ready to go to the polls, proud of my right to vote. But I think one of the sweetest victories has been to hear my sister-in-law say that all three of her children and their families are Democrats. Democrats! But why am I surprised? As I told her, she and her husband have smart children!

Ruth Coe Chambers

The Year My Mother Voted Democrat

I'm the only Democrat in my family. When the conversation turns to politics, I know I'll be glanced at condescendingly and baited by such jokes as my sister naming her dog Clinton "because he's taxing." To them, my liberalism reveals a lapse of common sense. They never stop hoping I'll "grow out of it." To me, their conservatism betrays a disappointing absence of generosity. And I don't understand why they've never noticed that it's their way of thinking that I have grown out of—inspired by the actions of our very conservative mother. Before I was ten years old, I was a knee-jerk Republican like them. After all, our father was a career Army officer, and the Republican Party "liked the military," as our mother put it. One of my earliest memories is of parading around the living room, chanting, "I Like Ike" during General Eisenhower's presidential campaign.

His name made me think of ice cream, and that little red, white, and blue "Ike and Nixon" campaign button was my most treasured possession for a few months. The thrill of the November day I woke up to learn that Eisenhower had won the election was more intense than Christmas morning. Although our father quietly judged many Democratic politicians "demagogues"—I can still hear him explaining that word to us—it was Mother who led the family on political issues. She was the staunch Republican of the two—even though New Deal programs had helped her learn to walk again after she survived polio as a young woman. With no consciousness of the political implications of her story, she would relate how desperate she had been to pay for her medical treatment, until a jovial nurse assured her that "Mr. Roosevelt's March of Dimes" would cover the costs.

My steadfastly Republican mother never made the logical next step from beneficiary of Democratic programs to supporter of the Democratic Party. But then came 1960, when Republican Richard Nixon ran for president against Democrat John F. Kennedy. Part of it was that Mother never did like Vice President Nixon—"tricky Dick"—whose shifty eyes and unshaven five o'clock shadow did not inspire trust. And Nixon's wife, Pat, was "bland" in Mother's view, while Jackie Kennedy brought an unprecedented stylishness to the campaign trail. Mother would still have backed her Republican candidate, though, if it hadn't been for people who made an issue of Senator Kennedy's Catholicism. Catholics, the argument went, took orders from the Pope in Rome. A Catholic couldn't really be a loyal American, let alone president. As Catholics back then, of course, we knew we weren't quite normal. Indeed, characters in popular books or on TV were routinely presumed to be Protestant. Still, it was a shock to me that many Americans thought of us as foreigners. But Mother wasn't surprised; she was angry. Even though she was not a regular at Mass on Sundays, she felt Catholic to the core, and she wasn't going to let anyone look down on us. By election day, her mind was made up.

That year she was proud to be one of the millions who pulled the lever for the Democratic candidate and elected JFK, the first Catholic president. And as I observed her righteous satisfaction at that victory, my childhood allegiance to Republicanism cracked imperceptibly. Over the next few years, I went to junior high school while President Kennedy explored a "New Frontier" of altruism, founded the Peace Corps to extend a helping hand to the world's poor, and denounced racial discrimination. My devotion to the principles of the Democratic Party took root.

I wish I could say that ever since the Kennedy administration my mother and I have lived arm-in-arm as fellow Democrats. The truth is, at age eighty-four, she considers herself an independent voter, but since 1960 she hasn't supported a presidential candidate who wasn't Republican. I continue to see the Republican Party as the stronghold of wealthy, corrupt insiders who manipulate otherwise decent, hard-working people. She considers the Democratic Party the breeding ground of naive, promiscuous eggheads. And from time to time, she'll ask me—in all seriousness—whether I've "come around" to voting Republican. When I opt for a quiet "No, and actually I don't plan to," she never fails to be surprised.

Mary Lash

WHO SAID IT?

"Conformity is the jailor of freedom and the enemy of growth."
—*John F. Kennedy*

"Washington is a very easy city for you to forget where you came from and why you got there in the first place."
—*Harry S. Truman*

"A man without a vote is man without protection."
—*Lyndon B. Johnson*

"We must stop thinking of the individual and start thinking about what is best for society."
—*Hillary Clinton*

"We must be the great arsenal of democracy."
—*Franklin Delano Roosevelt*

"The rain it raineth on the just and also on the unjust fella; but chiefly on the just, because the unjust steals the just's umbrella."
—*Sam Ervin*

"Freedom is the most contagious virus known to man."
—*Hubert Humphrey*

"The Constitution does not just protect those whose views we share; it also protects those with whose views we disagree."
—*Edward "Ted" Kennedy*

Mario Matthew Cuomo

1984 Democratic National Convention Keynote Address

"A Tale of Two Cities"

Delivered July 16, 1984 in San Francisco

Thank you very much.

On behalf of the great Empire State and the whole family of New York, let me thank you for the great privilege of being able to address this convention. Please allow me to skip the stories and the poetry and the temptation to deal in nice but vague rhetoric. Let me instead use this valuable opportunity to deal immediately with the questions that should determine this election and that we all know are vital to the American people.

Ten days ago, President Reagan admitted that although some people in this country seemed to be doing well nowadays, others were unhappy, even worried, about themselves, their families, and their futures. The President said that he didn't understand that fear. He said, "Why, this country is a shining city on a hill." And the President is right. In many ways we are a shining city on a hill.

But the hard truth is that not everyone is sharing in this city's splendor and glory. A shining city is perhaps all the President sees from the portico of the White House and the veranda of his ranch, where everyone seems to be doing well. But there's another city; there's another part to the shining the city; the part where some people can't pay their mortgages, and most young people can't afford one; where students can't afford the education they need, and middle-class parents watch the dreams they hold for their children evaporate.

In this part of the city there are more poor than ever, more families in trouble, more and more people who need help but can't find it. Even worse: There are elderly people who tremble in the basements of the houses there. And there are people who sleep in the city streets, in the gutter, where the glitter doesn't show. There are ghettos where thousands of young people, without a job or an education, give their lives away to drug dealers every day. There is despair, Mr. President, in the faces that you don't see, in the places that you don't visit in your shining city.

In fact, Mr. President, this is a nation—Mr. President you ought to know that this nation is more a "Tale of Two Cities" than it is just a "Shining City on a Hill."

Maybe, maybe, Mr. President, if you visited some more places; maybe if you went to Appalachia where some people still live in sheds; maybe if you went to Lackawanna where thousands of unemployed steel workers wonder why we subsidized foreign steel. Maybe— Maybe, Mr. President, if you stopped in at a shelter in Chicago and spoke to the homeless there; maybe, Mr. President, if you asked a woman who had been denied the help she needed to feed her children because you said you needed the money for a tax break for a millionaire or for a missile we couldn't afford to use.

Maybe—Maybe, Mr. President. But I'm afraid not. Because the

truth is, ladies and gentlemen, that this is how we were warned it would be. President Reagan told us from the very beginning that he believed in a kind of social Darwinism. Survival of the fittest. "Government can't do everything," we were told, so it should settle for taking care of the strong and hope that economic ambition and charity will do the rest. Make the rich richer, and what falls from the table will be enough for the middle class and those who are trying desperately to work their way into the middle class.

You know, the Republicans called it "trickle-down" when Hoover tried it. Now they call it "supply side." But it's the same shining city for those relative few who are lucky enough to live in its good neighborhoods. But for the people who are excluded, for the people who are locked out, all they can do is stare from a distance at that city's glimmering towers.

It's an old story. It's as old as our history. The difference between Democrats and Republicans has always been measured in courage and confidence. The Republicans—The Republicans believe that the wagon train will not make it to the frontier unless some of the old, some of the young, some of the weak are left behind by the side of the trail. "The strong"—"The strong," they tell us, "will inherit the land."

We Democrats believe in something else. We Democrats believe that we can make it all the way with the whole family intact, and we have more than once. Ever since Franklin Roosevelt lifted himself from his wheelchair to lift this nation from its knees—wagon train after wagon train—to new frontiers of education, housing, peace; the whole family aboard, constantly reaching out to extend and enlarge that family; lifting them up into the wagon on the way; blacks and Hispanics, and people of every ethnic group, and native Americans—all those struggling to build their families and claim some small share of America. For nearly fifty years we carried them all to new levels of comfort, and security, and dignity, even affluence. And remember this, some of us in this room today are here only because this nation had that kind of confidence. And it would be wrong to forget that.

So, here we are at this convention to remind ourselves where we come from and to claim the future for ourselves and for our children. Today our great Democratic Party, which has saved this nation from depression, from fascism, from racism, from corruption, is called upon to do it again—this time to save the nation from confusion and division, from the threat of eventual fiscal disaster, and most of all from the fear of a nuclear holocaust.

That's not going to be easy. Mo Udall is exactly right—it won't be easy. And in order to succeed, we must answer our opponent's polished and appealing rhetoric with a more telling reasonableness and rationality.

We must win this case on the merits. We must get the American public to look past the glitter, beyond the showmanship to the reality, the hard substance of things. And we'll do it not so much with speeches that sound good as with speeches that are good and sound; not so much with speeches that will bring people to their feet as with speeches that will bring people to their senses. We must make—We must make the American people hear our "Tale of Two Cities." We must convince them that we don't have to settle for two cities, that we can have one city, indivisible, shining for all of its people.

Now, we will have no chance to do that if what comes out of this convention is a babel of arguing voices. If that's what's heard throughout the campaign, dissident sounds from all sides, we will have no chance to tell our message. To succeed we will have to surrender some small parts of our individual interests, to build a platform that we can all stand on, at once, and comfortably—proudly singing out. We need—We need a platform we can all agree to so that we can sing out the truth for the nation to hear, in chorus, its logic so clear and commanding that no slick Madison Avenue commercial, no amount of geniality, no martial music will be able to muffle the sound of the truth.

And we Democrats must unite. We Democrats must unite so that the entire nation can unite, because surely the Republicans won't bring this country together. Their policies divide the nation into the lucky and the left-out, into the royalty and the rabble. The Republicans are willing to treat that division as victory. They would cut this nation in half, into those temporarily better off and those worse off than before, and they would call that division recovery.

Now, we should not—we should not be embarrassed or dismayed or chagrined if the process of unifying is difficult, even wrenching at times. Remember that, unlike any other Party, we embrace men and women of every color, every creed, every orientation, every economic class. In our family are gathered everyone from the abject poor of Essex County in New York, to the enlightened affluent of the gold coasts at both ends of the nation. And in between is the heart of our constituency—the middle class, the people not rich enough to be worry-free, but not poor enough to be on welfare; the middle class—those people who work for a living because they have to, not because some psychiatrist told them it was a convenient way to fill the interval between birth and eternity. White collar and blue collar. Young professionals. Men and women in small business desperate for the capital and contracts that they need to prove their worth.

We speak for the minorities who have not yet entered the mainstream. We speak for ethnics who want to add their culture to the magnificent mosaic that is America. We speak—We speak for women who are indignant that this nation refuses to etch into its governmental commandments the simple rule "thou shalt not sin against equality," a rule so simple—

I was going to say, and I perhaps dare not but I will. It's a commandment so simple it can be spelled in three letters: E.R.A.

We speak—We speak for young people demanding an education and a future. We speak for senior citizens. We speak for senior citizens who are terrorized by the idea that their only security, their Social Security, is being threatened. We speak for millions of reasoning people fighting to preserve our environment from greed and from stupidity. And we speak for reasonable people who are fighting to preserve our very existence from a macho intransigence that refuses to make intelligent attempts to discuss the possibility of nuclear holocaust with our enemy. They refuse. They refuse, because they believe we can pile missiles so high that they will pierce the clouds and the sight of them will frighten our enemies into submission.

Now we're proud of this diversity as Democrats. We're grateful for it. We don't have to manufacture it the way the Republicans will next month in Dallas, by propping up mannequin delegates on the convention floor. But we, while we're proud of this diversity, we pay a price for it. The different people that we represent have different points of view. And sometimes they compete and even debate, and even argue. That's what our primaries were all about. But now the primaries are over and it is time, when we pick our candidates and our platform here, to lock arms and move into this campaign together.

If you need any more inspiration to put some small part of your own difference aside to create this consensus, then all you need to do is to reflect on what the Republican policy of divide and cajole has done to this land since 1980. Now the President has asked the American people to judge him on whether or not he's fulfilled the promises he made four years ago. I believe, as Democrats, we ought to accept that challenge. And just for a moment let us consider what he has said and what he's done.

Inflation—Inflation is down since 1980, but not because of the supply-side miracle promised to us by the President. Inflation was reduced the old-fashioned way: with a recession, the worst since 1932. Now how did we—We could have brought inflation down that way. How did he do it? 55,000 bankruptcies; two years of massive unemployment; 200,000 farmers and ranchers forced off the land; more homeless—more homeless than at any time since the Great Depression in 1932; more hungry, in this world of enormous affluence, the United States of America, more hungry; more poor, most of them women. And—And he paid one other thing, a nearly 200 billion dollar deficit threatening our future.

Now, we must make the American people understand this deficit because they don't. The President's deficit is a direct and dramatic repudiation of his promise in 1980 to balance the budget by 1983. How large is it? The deficit is the largest in the history of the universe. It—President Carter's last budget had a deficit less than one-third of this deficit. It is a deficit that, according to the President's own fiscal adviser, may grow to as much 300 billion dollars a year for "as far as the eye can see." And, ladies and gentlemen, it is a debt so large—that is almost one-half of the money we collect from the personal income tax each year goes just to pay the interest. It is a mortgage on our children's future that can be paid only in pain and that could bring this nation to its knees.

Now don't take my word for it—I'm a Democrat. Ask the Republican investment bankers on Wall Street what they think the chances of this recovery being permanent are. You see, if they're not too embarrassed to tell you the truth, they'll say that they're appalled and frightened by the President's deficit. Ask them what they think of our economy, now that it's been driven by the distorted value of the dollar back to its colonial condition. Now we're exporting agricultural products and importing manufactured ones. Ask those Republican investment bankers what they expect the rate of interest to be a year from now. And ask them—if they dare tell you the truth—you'll learn from them, what they predict for the inflation rate a year from now, because of the deficit.

Now, how important is this question of the deficit? Think about it practically: What chance would the Republican candidate have had in 1980 if he had told the American people that he intended to pay for his so-called economic recovery with bankruptcies, unemployment, more homeless, more hungry, and the largest government debt known to humankind? If he had told the voters in 1980 that truth, would American voters have signed the loan certificate for him on Election Day? Of course not! That was an election won under false pretenses. It was won with smoke and mirrors and illusions. And that's the kind of recovery we have now as well.

But what about foreign policy? They said that they would make us and the whole world safer. They say they have. By creating the largest defense budget in history, one that even they now admit is excessive—by escalating to a frenzy the nuclear arms race; by incendiary rhetoric; by refusing to discuss peace with our enemies; by the loss of 279 young Americans in Lebanon in pursuit of a plan and a policy that no one can find or describe.

We give money to Latin American governments that murder nuns, and then we lie about it. We have been less than zealous in support of our only real friend—it seems to me, in the Middle East—the one democracy there, our flesh and blood ally, the state of Israel. Our—Our policy—Our foreign policy drifts with no real direction, other than an hysterical commitment to an arms race that leads nowhere—if we're lucky. And if we're not, it could lead us into bankruptcy or war.

Of course we must have a strong defense! Of course Democrats are for a strong defense. Of course Democrats believe that there are times that we must stand and fight. And we have. Thousands of us have paid for freedom with our lives. But always—when this country has been at its best—our purposes were clear. Now they're not. Now our allies are as confused as our enemies. Now we have no real commitment to our friends or to our ideals—not to human rights, not to the refuseniks, not to Sakharov, not to Bishop Tutu and the others struggling for freedom in South Africa.

We—We have in the last few years spent more than we can afford. We have pounded our chests and made bold speeches. But we lost 279 young Americans in Lebanon and we live behind sand bags in Washington. How can anyone say that we are safer, stronger, or better?

That—That is the Republican record. That its disastrous quality is not more fully understood by the American people I can only attribute to the President's amiability and the failure by some to separate the salesman from the product.

And, now—now—now it's up to us. Now it's up to you and to me to make the case to America. And to remind Americans that if they are not happy with all that the President has done so far, they should consider how much worse it will be if he is left to his radical proclivities for another four years unrestrained. Unrestrained.

Now, if—if July—if July brings back Ann Gorsuch Burford—what can we expect of December? Where would—Where would another four years take us? Where would four years more take us? How much larger will the deficit be? How much deeper the cuts in programs for the struggling middle class and the poor to limit that deficit? How high will the interest rates be? How much more acid rain killing our forests and fouling our lakes?

And, ladies and gentlemen, please think of this—the nation must think of this: What kind of Supreme Court will we have?

Please. [beckons audience to settle down]

We—We must ask ourselves what kind of court and country will be fashioned by the man who believes in having government mandate people's religion and morality; the man who believes that trees pollute the environment; the man that believes that—that the laws against discrimination against people go too far; a man who threatens Social Security and Medicaid and help for the disabled. How high will we pile the missiles? How much deeper will the gulf be between us and our enemies? And, ladies and gentlemen, will four years more make meaner the spirit of the American people? This election will measure the record of the past four years. But more than that, it will answer the question of what kind of people we want to be.

We Democrats still have a dream. We still believe in this nation's future. And this is our answer to the question. This is our credo:

We believe in only the government we need, but we insist on all the government we need.

We believe in a government that is characterized by fairness and reasonableness, a reasonableness that goes beyond labels, that doesn't distort or promise to do things that we know we can't do.

We believe in a government strong enough to use words like "love" and "compassion" and smart enough to convert our noblest aspirations into practical realities.

We believe in encouraging the talented, but we believe that while survival of the fittest may be a good working description of the process of evolution, a government of humans should elevate itself to a higher order.

We—Our—Our government—Our government should be able to rise to the level where it can fill the gaps that are left by chance or by a wisdom we don't fully understand. We would rather have laws written by the patron of this great city, the man called the "world's most sincere Democrat," St. Francis of Assisi, than laws written by Darwin.

We believe—We believe as Democrats, that a society as blessed as ours, the most affluent democracy in the world's history, one that can spend trillions on instruments of destruction, ought to be able to help the middle class in its struggle, ought to be able to find work for all who can do it, room at the table, shelter for the homeless, care for the elderly and infirm, and hope for the destitute. And we proclaim as loudly as we can the utter insanity of nuclear proliferation and the need for a nuclear freeze, if only to affirm the simple truth that peace is better than war because life is better than death.

We believe in firm—We believe in firm but fair law and order.

We believe proudly in the union movement.

We believe in a—We believe—We believe in privacy for people, openness by government.

We believe in civil rights, and we believe in human rights.

We believe in a single—We believe in a single fundamental idea that describes better than most textbooks and any speech that I could write what a proper government should be: the idea of family, mutuality, the sharing of benefits and burdens for the good of all, feeling one another's pain, sharing one another's blessings—reasonably, honestly, fairly, without respect to race, or sex, or geography, or political affiliation.

We believe we must be the family of America, recognizing that at the heart of the matter we are bound one to another, that the problems of a retired school teacher in Duluth are our problems; that the future of the child—that the future of the child in Buffalo is our future; that the struggle of a disabled man in Boston to survive and live decently is our struggle; that the hunger of a woman in Little Rock is our hunger; that the failure anywhere to provide what reasonably we might, to avoid pain, is our failure.

Now for fifty years—for fifty years we Democrats created a better future for our children, using traditional Democratic principles as a fixed beacon, giving us direction and purpose, but constantly innovating, adapting to new realities: Roosevelt's alphabet programs; Truman's NATO and the GI Bill of Rights; Kennedy's intelligent tax incentives and the Alliance for Progress; Johnson's civil rights; Carter's human rights and the nearly miraculous Camp David Peace Accord.

Democrats did it—Democrats did it, and Democrats can do it again. We can build a future that deals with our deficit. Remember this, that fifty years of progress under our principles never cost us what the last four years of stagnation have. And we can deal with the deficit intelligently, by shared sacrifice, with all parts of the nation's family contributing, building partnerships with the private sector, providing a sound defense without depriving ourselves of what we need to feed our children and care for our people. We can have a future that provides for all the young of the present, by marrying common sense and compassion.

We know we can, because we did it for nearly fifty years before 1980. And we can do it again, if we do not forget—if we do not forget that this entire nation has profited by these progressive principles; that they helped lift up generations to the middle class and higher; that they gave us a chance to work, to go to college, to raise a family, to own a house, to be secure in our old age and, before that, to reach heights that our own parents would not have dared dream of.

That struggle to live with dignity is the real story of the shining city. And it's a story, ladies and gentlemen, that I didn't read in a book, or learn in a classroom. I saw it and lived it, like many of you. I watched a small man with thick calluses on both his hands work fifteen and sixteen hours a day. I saw him once literally bleed from the bottoms of his feet, a man who came here uneducated, alone, unable to speak the language, who taught me all I needed to know about faith and hard work by the simple eloquence of his example. I learned about our kind of democracy from my father. And I learned about our obligation to each other from him and from my mother. They asked only for a chance to work and to make the world better for their children, and they—they asked to be protected in those moments when they would not be able to protect themselves. This nation and this nation's government did that for them.

And that they were able to build a family and live in dignity and see one of their children go from behind their little grocery store in South

Jamaica on the other side of the tracks where he was born, to occupy the highest seat, in the greatest State, in the greatest nation, in the only world we would know, is an ineffably beautiful tribute to the democratic process.

And—And, ladies and gentlemen, on January 20, 1985, it will happen again—only on a much, much grander scale. We will have a new President of the United States, a Democrat born not to the blood of kings but to the blood of pioneers and immigrants. And we will have America's first woman Vice President, the child of immigrants, and she—she—she will open with one magnificent stroke, a whole new frontier for the United States.

Now, it will happen. It will happen if we make it happen; if you and I make it happen. And I ask you now, ladies and gentlemen, brothers and sisters, for the good of all of us, for the love of this great nation, for the family of America, for the love of God: please, make this nation remember how futures are built.

Thank you and God bless you.

A great moment in Democratic history: Dr. Martin Luther King congratulates President Lyndon Baines Johnson at the signing of the 1964 Civil Rights Act.

Trivia

1. When was the Democratic National Committee formed?

2. Who were the only men to serve as vice presidents to two different presidents?

3. Who was the first woman elected to the Senate?

4. Who was the youngest man to serve as vice president?

5. Who was the only vice president to be administered the oath of office outside the United States?

6. Who was the first president to be born as a United States citizen?

7. Which president made the most trips outside the country?

8. Which presidents got married while in office?

9. When were Democrats popularly known as "Republicans"?

10. Which major wars of the twentieth century began during Democratic administrations?

1. The Democratic National Committee was created in 1848 to handle correspondence and raise and allocate campaign funds.
2. George Clinton served as vice president under Thomas Jefferson, 1805–1809, and James Madison, 1809–1812. John C. Calhoun served as vice president under John Quincy Adams, 1825–1829, and Andrew Jackson, 1829–1832.
3. Hattie Ophelia Wyatt Caraway was appointed to fill the vacancy caused by her husband's death in 1931. In 1932, she was elected to the first of two terms as senator from Arkansas.
4. John Cabell Breckinridge was thirty-six when he was sworn in as James Buchanan's vice president in 1857. He was only thirty-nine when he ran for the presidency as the candidate of the Southern Democrats in 1860.
5. William Rufus De Vane King, the running mate of Franklin Pierce. Seriously ill, King was administered the oath of office in Havana, Cuba, on March 4, 1853, after this had been authorized by a special act of Congress. He died in Alabama on April 18, after having served only twenty-five days as vice president.
6. Martin Van Buren, born December 5, 1782
7. William Jefferson Clinton, 133
8. Grover Cleveland and Woodrow Wilson
9. After Thomas Jefferson organized the first Democratic-Republican Societies, members were called Republicans.
10. World War I, Woodrow Wilson; World War II, Franklin Delano Roosevelt; Korean War, Harry S. Truman; Vietnam War, Lyndon Baines Johnson

Democrat or Republican?

When my daughter, Lynda, was in a senior civics class, she started questioning her parents' political thinking. We had some very thought-provoking and controversial political discussions.

"Mom, have you really thought about why you are still a registered Republican? I bet you have not processed this, and just because you were brought up in a Republican family, you have not even bothered to think about why." She was right.

I was brought up in a very conservative environment. My parents were registered Republicans. My father was an opinionated and prejudiced person and had no qualms about criticizing anyone whose thinking was different from his. He found fault with divorce, Catholics, Jews, blacks, and especially Democrats. This is part of my midwestern heritage.

We lived on a farm in central Minnesota during the Depression. We did not go hungry like many people in our country; we were fairly self-sufficient. However, we did not enjoy the luxury of running water, electricity, or telephone service. (Sometimes ignorance is bliss!)

I remember that my father was unhappy when Franklin Delano Roosevelt was elected in 1932. Dad did not appreciate Roosevelt's New Deal programs. Being only eight at that time, my memory is a bit hazy about the subject. I do remember my family sitting around my brother's homemade crystal radio set listening to Roosevelt's

Fireside Chats. I thought the president's voice was very comforting and supporting. I liked to listen to him.

In retrospect, my father did not appreciate the difficult problems the new president faced. Later, I read several history books on the subject and learned that the government was suffering from a legislative paralysis between the 1932 election and the following March inauguration. There was economic panic around the country and bewildering uncertainties concerning the world: Hitler's rising power, Japan's competing with the Western market, and the big question mark about the Soviet Union. In Roosevelt's first inaugural address, these grave concerns prompted his famous words, "The only thing we have to fear is fear itself."

My father continued to ridicule the Work Public Administration (WPA) and the Civilian Conservation Corps (CCC) programs. I felt badly about this because some of my friends' fathers were working for the WPA and CCC.

I was twelve years old in 1936, and so I remember more about Roosevelt's reelection. Many of his reform measures gradually lost their "terrifying" aspect after they were in place. The result was that the nation gained confidence and began to climb back to economic stability and prosperity.

It wasn't until I left home to attend the University of Minnesota that I started to question my father's close-minded views. In fact, I became angry with him for imprinting those views on my mind as a child. Later, after I matured, I was able to forgive him because I really tried to understand where he was coming from.

I remained a registered Republican until the mid-seventies. I remember the day I filled out the Democratic registration form at

Livermore City Hall. Many thoughts ran through my mind. *Why did I have this uncomfortable, guilty feeling about registering as a Democrat? It was just a form. Was I being disloyal to my Republican family? I would need to have a conversation with my father, but would he be able to hear my reasoning? Could I possibly change his thinking? Very unlikely!*

I finally decided to remain a Democrat. The only benefit in remaining Republican was that I had enjoyed voting in the primaries for the Republican candidate most likely to lose in the fall elections.

Audrey Lovell

A Grand Lady in Disguise

Like many high school students in the sixties, I was more interested in the latest Sonny and Cher song than in politics. I memorized pertinent facts for history, civics, and current events classes, but after I received a passing grade, my brain released the information, and I restocked it with rock-and-roll trivia. I was lucky I could remember the three branches of government; their respective duties were irrelevant to me.

When I became eligible to vote, I was more wrapped up in parenting issues than local politics, and national concerns were lower on my list than dusting, so I didn't even register. My thinking was flawed; I believed that my measly vote wouldn't make a difference. I listened to my parents complain about one politician or the other, harp about social issues and national concerns, but just like them, I allowed someone else to shoulder the burden. I stood proud as an American, but I bowed my head in shame when someone asked who I voted for in the presidential elections.

I listened to Republicans and Democrats alike run smear campaigns against one another. Radicals, moderates, liberals, and conservatives blasted each other in public arenas. Independents swayed me on some issues, but not enough to earn my vote. It wasn't that I didn't have an opinion or that I was easily persuaded; it was simply that the issues didn't touch my daily life. If any of the politicians could have produced a better diaper, or a pacifier that didn't have to be retrieved off the floor at night, I'd have probably headed up his or her campaign. As I grew older, I listened to the rhetoric, but I weighed issues on a scale of how I would be affected. Usually in the grand scheme of things, my lifestyle wouldn't be altered, so I didn't get politically involved. That is, until my former husband, a union tradesman, came home riled up about the possibility of losing his job to underskilled workers willing to perform his tasks for considerably less than a union wage. This issue would definitely affect my standard of living. I joined throngs of Missourians who fought long and hard on behalf of labor unions so that our state would not become a right-to-work state. I registered to vote in the presidential election, stumped for former president Bill Clinton, and badgered family and friends to cast their votes for the Democrats who represented the working class.

I did my research and discovered that the Republican platform, in general, was based on the premise that government should be less involved in social programs; the party encouraged personal financial responsibility. Some Democrats and many Republicans were more concerned with moral issues than economics, and were opposed to universal health care. They believed there should be a safety net for elderly and indigent Americans, but the net was threadbare in our state. I'd seen how poverty affected my own relatives. I was confused. I was frustrated when a Republican administration overstepped its power, but I felt powerless to effect change.

I rejoiced when the Democrats of the 110th U.S. Congress took back the House of Representatives and the Senate after the 2006 midterm elections. I anticipated sweeping changes. The first change that affected *my* house was when our Republican governor made drastic social and welfare cuts that targeted senior citizens.

One day I went to pick up my white-haired mother, and I barely recognized her. I was shocked to see that she had colored her hair.

"I can't afford the permanent stuff, but I bought a bottle of shampoo-in color rinse," she told me.

"Why, Mom?" I asked. She'd given up coloring her hair twenty years earlier.

"Honey, I heard that senior citizens who go to the hospitals or have to get prescriptions or need financial help will have trouble getting these services with these budget cuts. Churches are supposed to help us out, but I thought that's what Social Security was for. I colored my hair so I won't look so old. I don't want to be treated unfairly because of my age. We are already discriminated against as it is, but the news says it's going to get worse."

Mom wasn't mentally deficient; she was simply worried.

I mounted a letter-writing campaign; I advocated for my elderly parents whose fixed income, like many of their friends', was below poverty level. I spoke on behalf of those whose voices are heard but seldom listened to. I voted in every election because I discovered my measly vote does count. In almost six decades, I have learned a lot about our country and political system.

I have been a pre-kindergarten teacher for more than thirty years. Ever since I was a kindergarten student myself, I have always stopped respectfully in my tracks whenever the national anthem pealed over school intercoms. I placed my hand over my heart, and I recited the Pledge of Allegiance. Like the rest of America's children, I was indoctrinated to believe in patriotism and democracy. I was taught that the U.S. Constitution was designed for the people and by the people—with liberty and justice for all. I now believe that our country is no longer being governed "by the people and for the people." It is being run by big business for big business. Whether voters lean to the left or to the right, or whether they straddle the proverbial fence, it is time for the people to take back America, take back "liberty and justice"— not for the poor, not for the wealthy, but for all. United we *must* stand, and let our collective democratic voices be heard.

Linda O'Connell

"Don't be a sore loser," said Miss Mary Bill Allison. "You ran a clean race and gave it your best shot. Don't call for a recount of votes." I thanked Mary Bill and hung up the phone. Tears streamed down my face as I recalled the race for school board in Clay County, North Carolina. I had almost won as a Democratic candidate, but "almost" wasn't good enough. No matter how many people tried to console me, it really hurt to lose an election. Guilt and self-condemnation smothered me like a black curtain. I shouldn't have run for school board. I just made a fool of myself and ruined my reputation.

As a Christian, I had no business getting involved with politics. My daddy was a Baptist preacher and instilled conservative Christian values in me, but my family still held on to our southern roots. My relatives had been Democrats since the Civil War and did not change politics when the southern states went red. My granny Trese Lee was a strong Democrat. She often recalled how President Franklin D. Roosevelt saved her children from starvation during the Great Depression.

She had a photo of FDR in her and Granddaddy's bedroom. She declared, "When I die, just write 'Democrat' on my tombstone." Aunt Mary Lou Auberry was also a staunch Democrat. I often attended political rallies with her. She was very vocal regarding her political views. The federal government convicted her son of buying votes for the Democrats during the 1980s. He and two former sheriffs, one a

Democrat and one a Republican, served time in prison for buying votes in Clay County. After the FBI conducted the investigation into voting fraud, people were wary of politics here in the mountains of western North Carolina. No one would file for the Democratic ticket.

Late one Friday evening, the chairman of the Democratic Party called. "Brenda, we need you to run for school board. Everyone is afraid to run for office after the investigation. If someone doesn't file, it will automatically go to the Republicans."

"Well, George, I don't have time to run for school board. I'm a teacher in Cherokee County, and I have no energy for extra duties."

"But that's why we need you," insisted George. "You're the most qualified person for the ticket. You're a teacher and a good Democrat."

"I don't know, George. I'll let you know."

"We need to know by Monday," he said. "The filing closes then."

I promised I would pray about running for school board and let him know before the deadline. I sought God's guidance. I wanted to serve him and be faithful as a disciple of Christ. Many churches in Clay County were conservative. I had a lot of Republican friends and didn't want to offend them by running for a political office. Until that moment, I had never become involved with politics. How could I declare myself a Democrat and remain a conservative Christian? Did my values clash with the Democratic ideas? I asked the pastor of Truett Memorial Baptist Church what he thought about my filing for school board. Rev. Chester Jones was a registered Republican and a personal friend. He told me, "It would be hard, but we need good people in politics." I decided to run for school board. I had the desire to help the children, serve the community, and take a stand for Christ by running on the Democratic ticket.

As a teacher, I had always voted for the candidates who supported education. I belonged to the North Carolina Association of Educators. Usually, NCAE endorsed Democrats because they promoted public education. Besides supporting education, the Democratic Party cares for the underprivileged, minorities, senior citizens, health issues, women, the environment, and children. Democrats believe in treating all people equally and not favoring the rich. When Christ was on Earth, he ate with tax collectors and Pharisees. He witnessed to prostitutes and Samaritans. He healed those with leprosy and loved those cast out by society. This sounds like the ideology of the Democratic Party to me. So being a conservative Christian does not conflict with my political affiliation. Of course, God is not a Democrat or a Republican. He loves everyone equally.

In the end, I felt obligated to run on the Democratic ticket for school board. Clay County was still in turmoil after the voter fraud investigation. Politics divided the little county, and a lot of folks wanted to get even with the opposite party. I didn't realize how crooked politics could be, especially in the mountains of western North Carolina. I almost lost my job teaching when I filed for school board. One day, my principal called me aside. "Miss Ledford, someone reported you to the superintendent and told him to fire you because you're running for school board on the Democratic ticket. He refused to fire you because of your politics."

The rancor ran even deeper. The Republican Party placed an ad in the local newspaper right before the election, when it was too late to write a rebuttal in the paper. The ad stated that a single woman, a teacher in the adjacent county, was running for school board and was not qualified for the office. I attended a political rally that evening.

When I gave my speech, I let the people know my view regarding the ad. "It's not your marital status that qualifies a person to run for school board. You don't have to bear children to care for them. Jesus Christ was single, but no one loved children more than Jesus. He said, 'Suffer the little children to come unto me for such is the Kingdom of God.'

"I'm a public-school teacher because I love children. Our young people are our future. I'm a lifetime Democrat and proud of it. That's why I'm running for school board." After my speech, I received a standing ovation. Burnace Roberts, the University director of NCAE, attended the meeting. He told me, "Brenda, you are one hell of a speaker!" Although I lost the election for school board, I learned a lot. Don't judge people by their politics. We have many fine people in America, both Democrats and Republicans.

Brenda Kay Ledford

The Birth of a Democrat

My grandfather, Francis S. Lorenz, was an active Democratic politician for fifty-six years. He was Cook County treasurer, Illinois state treasurer, director of public works, clerk of the circuit court, and, finally, chief appellate court justice. Because of him, my first taste of politics came while sitting in my grandparents' den, flipping through dusty albums of old photographs and newspaper clippings.

There were pictures of my grandfather with other politicians, socialites, and presidents, and articles from speeches he gave or projects he had done. Naturally, politics often came up during dinner conversations throughout my childhood years. When I was younger, it seemed politics was always overdiscussed, very boring. As I grew older, however, and started defining who I was, my own political beliefs became well integrated into the shape of my character.

I frequently heard my grandfather talk about politics, but not in the way that is popular today. There were talks of labor, work, and people's faith in their representatives. When I was old enough to vote, I realized that I had to decide where I belonged on the political spectrum. My family, although almost entirely Democratic, never once pressured me to pick a certain affiliation. They left that decision solely to me.

High school was where I learned exactly how I felt about certain topics—those tough issues that naturally surround the political arena.

Whenever a political question came up, I questioned myself about it. It was interesting to see that almost all my opinions fell along the "left side." By my senior year, I was tremendously confident and passionate about my personal beliefs on controversial subjects, and I greatly enjoyed debating them with others.

My choice to become a Democrat, however, was based on a much more profound influence. The more I learned about the way Democracy worked, the more I liked it. While attending a Democratic dinner with my grandfather, I read a quote from Thomas Jefferson that helped define my political beliefs more than anything else: "I have sworn upon the altar of God eternal hostility against every form of tyranny over the mind of man." After I really gave those words some thought, I truly felt a deep connection to my party. I realized I was really a Democrat, not because of opinion or influence, but in my heart.

During November of my eighteenth year, my parents took me to the polls to vote for the very first time. They didn't tell me who to vote for; they only told me to vote because it was my right.

It hasn't always been easy being a Democrat. I have done my best, though, to show that Democrats are not nonreligious or immoral— an untrue accusation that's often thrown at us. I try to show people that it's possible to be a religious Democrat, and because I am Catholic, that's not always easy when you are sometimes surrounded by people who feel differently than you about some things.

I will always remember my grandfather telling me something that his own father said to him when he graduated from law school. He told my grandfather, "You were born poor. We were all born poor. No matter where you go or how much you make, remember where you came from. Remember that you were poor." My grandfather obeyed his father's wise words. Even though he went on to be very successful and made quite a fine living, he remained deeply rooted in his Democratic beliefs.

I have an innate love for this country and the principles it was founded on: escaping tyranny, freedom of faith, and a voice for all citizens. I care deeply for those who don't have enough. For me, being a Democrat is not about criticizing the rich and throwing money into the streets. It's about opening our minds; about daring to dream for a better tomorrow; about believing in a world where the *people* have the loudest voice and nurture a glorious country founded on ideas worth celebrating. A world where the rich man bends down to help the poor man up. A world where those who have enough help those who don't. A world where social standing is obsolete.

I once heard someone say, "America did not invent human rights; human rights invented America." I think that if we lead our country with our hearts instead of our wallets that peace may be more easily achieved. I believe that if we nurture our country with compassion for all, not just the wealthy and powerful, if we learn to appreciate other religious beliefs and lifestyles, and if we treat others fairly, despite economic standing, we may re-create the country and better life that our Founding Fathers envisioned, and the liberty and equality they foresaw for all people.

Katelyn Lorenz

WHO SAID IT?

"Forgive your enemies but never forget their names."

—*John F. Kennedy*

"The only thing we have to fear is fear itself."

—*Franklin Delano Roosevelt*

"The buck stops here."

—*Harry S. Truman*

"A good Republican is one who doesn't want anybody to know it."

—*James Carville*

"No one can make
you feel inferior
without your consent."
—Eleanor Roosevelt

"America must be a light to the
world, not just a missile."
—Nancy Pelosi

"To the victor
belong the spoils."
—William Marcy

"The ugliness of bigotry
stands in dircot contradiction
to the very meaning of America."
—Hubert Humphrey

William Jefferson Clinton
Oklahoma Bombing Memorial Prayer Service Address
Delivered April 23, 1995, in Oklahoma City, OK

Thank you very much, Governor Keating and Mrs. Keating, Reverend Graham, to the families of those who have been lost and wounded, to the people of Oklahoma City, who have endured so much, and the people of this wonderful state, to all of you who are here as our fellow Americans.

I am honored to be here today to represent the American people. But I have to tell you that Hillary and I also come as parents, as husband and wife, as people who were your neighbors for some of the best years of our lives.

Today our nation joins with you in grief. We mourn with you. We share your hope against hope that some may still survive. We thank all those who have worked so heroically to save lives and to solve this crime—those here in Oklahoma and those who are all across this great land, and many who left their own lives to come here to work hand in hand with you. We pledge to do all we can to help you heal the injured, to rebuild this city, and to bring to justice those who did this evil.

This terrible sin took the lives of our American family, innocent children in that building, only because their parents were trying to be good parents as well as good workers; citizens in the building going about their daily business; and many there who served the rest of us—who worked to help the elderly and the disabled, who worked to support our farmers and our veterans, who worked to enforce our laws and to protect us. Let us say clearly, they served us well, and we are grateful.

But for so many of you they were also neighbors and friends. You saw them at church or the PTA meetings, at the civic clubs, at the ball park. You know them in ways that all the rest of America could not. And to all the members of the families here present who have suffered loss, though we share your grief, your pain is unimaginable, and we know that. We cannot undo it. That is God's work.

Our words seem small beside the loss you have endured. But I found a few I wanted to share today. I've received a lot of letters in these last terrible days.

One stood out because it came from a young widow and a mother of three whose own husband was murdered with over 200 other Americans when Pan Am 103 was shot down. Here is what that woman said I should say to you today:

"The anger you feel is valid, but you must not allow yourselves to be consumed by it. The hurt you feel must not be allowed to turn into hate, but instead into the search for justice. The loss you feel must not paralyze your own lives. Instead, you must try to pay tribute to your loved ones by continuing to do all the things they left undone, thus ensuring they did not die in vain."

Wise words from one who also knows.

You have lost too much, but you have not lost everything. And you have certainly not lost America, for we will stand with you for as many tomorrows as it takes.

If ever we needed evidence of that, I could only recall the words of Governor and Mrs. Keating: "If anybody thinks that Americans are mostly mean and selfish, they ought to come to Oklahoma. If anybody thinks Americans have lost the capacity for love and caring and courage, they ought to come to Oklahoma."

To all my fellow Americans beyond this hall, I say, one thing we owe those who have sacrificed is the duty to purge ourselves of the dark forces which gave rise to this evil. They are forces that threaten our common peace, our freedom, our way of life. Let us teach our children that the God of comfort is also the God of righteousness: those who trouble their own house will inherit the wind. Justice will prevail.

Let us let our own children know that we will stand against the forces of fear. When there is talk of hatred, let us stand up and talk against it. When there is talk of violence, let us stand up and talk against it. In the face of death, let us honor life. As St. Paul admonished us, let us "not be overcome by evil, but overcome evil with good."

Yesterday, Hillary and I had the privilege of speaking with some children of other federal employees—children like those who were lost here. And one little girl said something we will never forget. She said, "We should all plant a tree in memory of the children." So this morning before we got on the plane to come here, at the White House, we planted that tree in honor of the children of Oklahoma. It was a dogwood with its wonderful spring flower and its deep, enduring roots. It embodies the lesson of the Psalms—that the life of a good person is like a tree whose leaf does not wither.

My fellow Americans, a tree takes a long time to grow, and wounds take a long time to heal. But we must begin. Those who are lost now belong to God. Some day we will be with them. But until that happens, their legacy must be our lives.

Thank you all, and God bless you.

A great moment in Democratic history: March 26, 1979—President Jimmy Carter exults at the historic signing of the Israel-Egypt Peace Treaty with Egypt's Anwar Sadat and Israel's Menachem Begin, shaking hands in agreement.

Trivia

1. Who was the last man to be expelled for treason from the Senate?

2. Who was the only man to serve more than two terms as president?

3. Who was the youngest man to be elected president?

4. Who was the longest serving mayor of Chicago?

5. Who was the only Democratic Speaker of the House to become vice president?

6. Who was the shortest president?

7. When were the first televised presidential debates?

8. When did the "First Hundred Days" of a presidential term become symbolically important?

9. What is the origin of the term "gerrymander"?

10. What is a "Yellow Dog"?

1. Jesse Bright of Indiana was the only northerner to be forced from the Senate during the Civil War. In 1862, the Senate voted 32–14 to expel him after he provided a friend with a letter of introduction to Jefferson Davis, the President of the Confederate States of America.

2. Franklin Delano Roosevelt, elected 1932, 1936, 1940, and 1944, serving 1933–1945

3. John F. Kennedy in 1960

4. Richard J. Daley, was the mayor of Chicago from 1955–1976. He was regarded as the last of the big-city bosses. His son, Richard M. Daley, may surpass his record of longevity as mayor.

5. John Nance Garner of Texas was Speaker of the House, 1931–1933, and vice president, 1933–1941. Garner declared that the vice presidency was not worth "a bucket of warm spit."

6. James Madison at five feet, four inches

7. 1960, between John F. Kennedy and Richard M. Nixon

8. In his first 100 days in office, Franklin Delano Roosevelt sponsored a flurry of legislation inaugurating his New Deal. During this period, on March 12, 1933, Roosevelt gave his first radio "fireside chat" to the nation.

9. In 1812, Democratic-Republicans in the Massachusetts legislature created a politically safe district that looked like a salamander. After Governor Elbridge Gerry signed the legislation, politicized redistricting became known as "gerrymandering."

10. This term arose in the late 19th and early 20th centuries to describe southern Democrats who would vote for a "yaller dog" before a Republican. The term achieved national recognition in 1928, when Democrat Alfred E. Smith ran against Herbert Hoover.

Winning Hearts and Minds

The things I do for love . . . why else would I get up early on chilly Saturday mornings in mid-October to pound the pavement doing precinct work? Our assignment—technically, it was my new boyfriend Greg's assignment since I was just tagging along—was to go door to door in one of Chicago's northside working-class neighborhoods to ask registered Democratic voters if they would consider voting for a candidate who was running for a seat in the U.S. House of Representatives. The Democratic candidate's name was Rod Blagojevich, and his Eastern European surname was a clear indication that he was a Chicago native.

A brisk wind tugged at the changing leaves that were at the peak of their autumn colors, but not even the breeze could drown out the steady hum of weekend traffic on the Kennedy Expressway. Greg and I grabbed a handful of brochures from his car and began canvassing the neighborhood, using the voter registration records as our guide. We knew that we would have no problem finding Democratic voters in Chicago; the only thing I wondered was whether or not they wanted to be bothered with campaign literature on a Saturday morning. I secretly hoped that Greg appreciated my presence; even though I agreed with Blagojevich's platform and thought that he would be an effective congressman—I'd even met the man at a recent campaign function—I lived outside of his district and wouldn't be able to vote for him.

Making our way down the block of sturdy brick bungalows, Greg rang the doorbells of each house on the list while I clutched the brochures against my chest for extra warmth. If no one answered, we left behind a campaign flyer in the mailbox; if someone came to the door, Greg would introduce himself and the reason for our visit. I was impressed with the ease of Greg's presentation, and how he was able to briefly lay out where Blagojevich stood on the issues that were most pertinent to the residents of the neighborhood. I was equally pleased that all of the voters we talked to showed at least some degree of interest in our candidate's record, and that there was no angry feedback or slammed doors on this particular campaign trail.

After a few hours of canvassing the neighborhood, Greg and I dropped into a local diner. On Chicago's north side that meant a Greek-owned restaurant that displayed luscious cakes and cream pies in a glass case by the front cash register, and offered plenty of hot coffee in sturdy ceramic cups. Sitting in a booth at the restaurant, I waited until I felt the warmth of the coffee coursing through my body before asking Greg the question that had been on my mind all morning. "So, what motivates you to volunteer so much of your time to help Rod get elected?"

"I think he is the right man for the job, and he won't forget about the people here at home if he goes off to Washington, D.C.," Greg responded. "And, more than anything, I like being a part of the political process. I feel like I can make a difference in some way by helping these candidates get elected, because ultimately all of these public officials have to answer to voters like you and me."

Greg took another sip of his coffee before taking my hand in his across the table. "By the way," he added, "thanks for coming out here with me today. It's certainly a lot more fun getting the precinct work done when you're with me."

Blagojevich won the election and eventually became governor of Illinois. My precinct-canvassing boyfriend won my heart, and eventually became my husband and the father of my children.

Robyn Kurth

What Is a Democrat?

Fifty years ago, being a Democrat wasn't what it is today—at least not for this now sixty-eight-year-old woman. At our house, a Democrat was a steelworker, and his entire family was Democrats, too! Neither of my parents ever talked about the reasons our family were registered with the Democratic Party. As I got older, however, I knew it was because Dad was a union man. When it came time for me to vote, I got simple instructions from my mother. "You go in, shut the curtain, pull the lever by the sign that says Democrat, and leave." Never in my wildest dreams would I have considered doing anything else. In fact, as a young woman it felt good to be a Democratic. After all, isn't that what every country in the world wanted—democracy? So, even though my mom and dad didn't talk about why we were what we were, I certainly didn't ask. That's just the way it was back in the fifties. But my curiosity finally got to me. And, as I'd always done when I wasn't sure about something, I got out my trusty dictionary.

I started with Democrat. Sure enough, it was in there. The dictionary said *an adherent of democracy; one who practices social equality.* Sounded good enough for me, but I looked up democracy too, just to be sure. Democracy, according to the dictionary, was *a government by the people.* That cinched it. Finally, I knew why our family were Democrats.

I looked up republic and Republican too, just for fun. A republic, according to the dictionary, was *a government having a chief of state who is not a monarch.* A Republican was related to or had the charac-teristics of a republic, or constituted one of the two major U.S. polit-ical parties that evolved in the mid-nineteenth century.

And so, all those years ago, my status was confirmed. I knew with-out a doubt that I wanted to be a Democrat. I wanted a government by the people. I wanted to be an adherent of democracy (even though I'm not sure I knew what "adherent" meant back then!). I wanted to practice social equality. Who wouldn't? Not the Republicans, accord-ing to the dictionary.

Years passed. I married and had six children, a house, and a car. My husband and I were living the American dream, and during every election I went to the polls and voted a straight Democratic ticket. For many of those years, I had no idea that you could even split your vote and not pull that one lever!

Then it happened. One election year, I didn't like the guy who was running on the Democratic ticket. I didn't want him to be my president. So I did the unthinkable—I voted for the Republican candidate.

Today, in 2008, I can't even remember who it was! I'm grinning, of course, because I'm not sure I'd tell even if I did remember.

Actually, it doesn't matter. What matters is that I was suddenly a woman who did not vote the way my family had voted for genera-tions. To this day, I thank God I did not have to answer to my dad. We might have a talk about it when we meet in heaven one day, but for the time being, I was my own woman, with my own opinions.

Then came the presidential election when Al Gore was running against George Bush. I won't get into the "whys" at this point, but I had made my decision and was going to vote for Bush. Just as my parents before me, my husband and I never discussed who we were voting for. We talked about issues, maybe even argued just a little. But, head of the family that he was, my hubby "assumed" I was voting his way.

I will forever remember that voting day in November 2000. We were headed to the polls, using our back driveway, which cut between our house and our closest neighbors and dear friends. They happened to be outside as we drove by, and we stopped for a minute. My friend Darlene called out asking who we were voting for.

At the exact same moment, my husband said "Gore" and I said "Bush." He turned to me, his facial expression a mixture of horror and disbelief. "You're going to cancel out my vote?"

I shook my head. "No. You're canceling out my vote."

"We might as well not even go," he shouted, though he'd already put the car in drive and headed out to the road, leaving our neighbors behind with huge grins on their faces.

"How can you vote for Bush?" were his next words.

I stated a few of my reasons, and he just yelled louder. Even though we "discussed" our candidates for the next five minutes as we drove to the polls, I knew my opinion wouldn't change and his wouldn't either.

Despite the fact that we "canceled out" each other's vote, we *did* vote.

That's one of the most important rights we have in a democracy. We have a right to vote, and no one, not even an angry husband, has the right to stop us.

We did kiss and make up later, of course, and agreed never to talk politics again. What is that old saying? Politics makes strange bedfellows!

The funny thing about our presidential votes that year was the fact that my husband was a registered Republican and I remained a registered Democrat. Neither of us had voted for our party's candidate.

What a great country we live in!

God bless America!

Lorraine Henderson

A Tempest of Motivation

On a frosty February day, tens of thousands filled the grounds of the old state capitol in Springfield, Illinois, coming from all points of the Union to witness Senator Barack Obama announce his presidential candidacy.

Smiles danced on the crowd's faces, and hope shined in their eyes. Here was the man who, years earlier, called upon the nation to no longer be a house divided, red against blue, white against black—a message that had inspired me.

I threw caution to the wind, risking the chance that I would be late for work just to witness history. It's in my nature. I can't help it because I spent four years as a journalist, recording history. The thirst for witnessing history comes from my parents, both fierce Democrats. They took me to political meetings throughout my youth (whether I wanted to go or not), introducing me to leaders from then-Governor Bill Clinton to Senator Paul Simon to senatorial hopeful Carol Moseley Braun to then-state Senator Barack Obama.

When I first heard Obama speak to a crowd on Governor's Day 2003 at the Illinois State Fair, I did not know the influence he would have on me. Among a large field of Illinois senatorial primary candidates, he stood out—not because he was black, but because his message intrigued me. He called on Illinoisans to come together and have empathy for all.

I met him the night before the rally. His campaign greeted potential supporters in a room not much larger than a small bedroom—

not the grand ballroom or crowded bars the other candidates occupied. Obama's was a room where staffers and volunteers outnumbered the tiny trickle of possible followers.

My dad and I share one passion—politics; it gives us something to talk about and share as father and daughter. My father, a Democratic county chairman, had thrown his support behind the state's comptroller. So he could not endorse Obama, but Obama enthralled us enough to come back hours later just to talk politics and policies.

With my affinity for wanting to be close to the action, I pushed my way to the front of the state fair crowd to hear the candidates. I immediately knew Obama had my vote because his message was unique. It inspired me enough to intern for his campaign in the summer of 2004. I wanted to do my part to heal the wounds of my state and nation, to give the electorate more than a choice of the lesser of who cares, and to raise the level of public debate.

During my time in the Springfield office, Obama delivered the keynote address at the Democratic convention—the speech that launched him on the nation and asked citizens to unite in hope for a better America.

I remember it well. I couldn't go to the campaign's watch party, so I watched it from the house I was staying in. The eloquence stirred hearts deep in the souls of people, and emotions broke like waves through the crowd in Boston and in living rooms across the land. Tears flowed—not of sadness, but of inspiration and hope for a new day.

I am too young to remember John F. Kennedy. I only know him from books, television, and movies. I cannot claim I saw him campaign like my aunt did, and I cannot claim I watched his inaugural address when it was first televised like my baby boomer parents did. However, they did tell me about the sense of hope and inspiration that surrounded JFK. I was raised on Kennedy, though I cannot lay claim to him. But I can lay claim to the sense of being called to a higher purpose by Obama's speech.

I, too, wanted America to "reclaim its promise," have our nation get out of "this long political darkness," and hope that "a brighter day will come."

I, too, wanted to get past the red versus blue politics that has defined so much of the politics of the last decade. I, too, realized that "we worship an awesome God in the Blue States and we don't like federal agents poking around our libraries in the Red States. We coach Little League in the Blue States and, yes, we've got some gay friends in the Red States."

I, too, wanted be the "United States of America" again and celebrate that we can each "pursue our individual dreams and yet still come together as one American family" to solve problems.

I, too, believed that "when a child in the south side of Chicago can't read, it matters to me even if it's not my child." And I believed we should be united as a people in facing our problems.

The speech summed up all the reasons to be a Democrat, and even if one was a Republican or an Independent, it spelled out all the reasons not to be a divided people. I wanted to aid that factory worker who lost his job, the student who couldn't afford college, the victims of natural disasters who needed a helping hand.

That was one speech, four years ago. The message, however, is still the same, even on a wintry day in February. I try to heed the call to work together and achieve success. I try to do my part and inspire others to do the same, all because of a speech that spawned a tempest of motivation to get the populace off their couches and do something for their country.

Tracy Douglas

Seeing Differences

The lesson stuck like gum to a sneaker's sole—not comfortable to walk on, and annoying to have stepped in. But step in it, I did. It started simply enough as a civics lesson on the democratic process. We lined up, waiting our turn to enter the voting booth to mark our sample presidential ballots. Unlike a nation waiting late into the evening to discover if Nixon or Kennedy would be the next White House resident, we knew after lunch how the fifth grade at Liberty School voted.

And then it happened. The person I voted for narrowly lost. How could that be? These were my friends and classmates. I knew them. How was it they didn't think like me? Or rather, how was it that their parents didn't think like my parents?

By afternoon recess, the sides were drawn. Debater in my blood, I led arguments over whose vote was right. I redefined friends as the ones who thought like me. The normal walk-home-together crowd was split into two groups, one trailing behind the other on the dusty trek across the playground. That election changed me. Now, I saw our differences.

Of course, not for long. It *was* fifth grade. I didn't understand or care about politics at ten. But, like hardened gum molded to my sneaker's sole, its residue remained. More differences emerged as we passed from grade to grade. Differences divided us—the jocks and the eggheads, the partiers and the Pollyannas, the debate team and the car club. Today, adult-size issues divide a class that started kindergarten together—issues like the environment, guns, abortion, religion, politics, and war.

In fact, one close friend and I are so different in how we orient to the world that we stopped discussing politics and religion altogether. Yet we are similar souls. We want a better life for our children. We want a safer, peaceful, prosperous world for our grandchildren. We want the same things; we just see how to get them differently.

It's funny. Now all grown up, the differences don't matter as much. I'm a Democrat, but I have Democrat and Republican friends; friends who carry guns and friends who find them abhorrent; friends who have fought in war and friends who marched against it. I don't pick my friends anymore for thinking like me. I pick them for their hearts.

I can see philosophical differences between us. I can also see and feel our similarities. For me, in the scheme of things, your good nature will trump our thought differences, any day. Kind. Loving. Giving. Honorable. It's your actions that speak to my heart.

Nan Schindler Russell

WHO SAID IT?

"The ignorance of one voter in a democracy impairs the security of all."

—*John F. Kennedy*

"America did not invent human rights. In a very real sense, it is the other way around. Human rights invented America."

—*Jimmy Carter*

"If you can't stand the heat, get out of the kitchen."

—*Harry Truman*

"No matter how hard the loss, defeat might serve as well as victory to shake the soul and let the glory out."

—*Al Gore*

Thank you so much. Thank you. Thank you. Thank you so much. Thank you so much. Thank you. Thank you. Thank you, Dick Durbin. You make us all proud.

On behalf of the great state of Illinois, crossroads of a nation, Land of Lincoln, let me express my deepest gratitude for the privilege of addressing this convention.

Tonight is a particular honor for me because, let's face it, my presence on this stage is pretty unlikely. My father was a foreign student, born and raised in a small village in Kenya. He grew up herding goats, went to school in a tin-roof shack. His father—my grandfather—was a cook, a domestic servant to the British.

But my grandfather had larger dreams for his son. Through hard work and perseverance my father got a scholarship to study in a magical place, America, that shone as a beacon of freedom and opportunity to so many who had come before.

While studying here, my father met my mother. She was born in a town on the other side of the world, in Kansas. Her father worked on oil rigs and farms through most of the Depression. The day after Pearl Harbor, my grandfather signed up for duty, joined Patton's army, marched across Europe. Back home, my grandmother raised a baby and went to work on a bomber assembly line. After the war, they studied on the GI Bill, bought a house through FHA, and later moved west all the way to Hawaii in search of opportunity.

And they, too, had big dreams for their daughter. A common dream, born of two continents.

My parents shared not only an improbable love; they shared an abiding faith in the possibilities of this nation. They would give me an African name, Barack, or "blessed," believing that in a tolerant America your name is no barrier to success. They imagined—They imagined me going to the best schools in the land, even though they weren't rich, because in a generous America you don't have to be rich to achieve your potential.

They're both passed away now. And yet, I know that on this night they look down on me with great pride.

They stand here—And I stand here today, grateful for the diversity of my heritage, aware that my parents' dreams live on in my two precious daughters. I stand here knowing that my story is part of the larger American story, that I owe a debt to all of those who came before me, and that, in no other country on eEarth, is my story even possible.

Tonight, we gather to affirm the greatness of our nation—not because of the height of our skyscrapers, or the power of our military, or the size of our economy. Our pride is based on a very simple premise, summed up in a declaration made over two hundred years ago:

We hold these truths to be self-evident, that all men are created equal, that they are endowed by their Creator with certain inalienable rights, that among these are Life, Liberty and the pursuit of Happiness.

That is the true genius of America, a faith—a faith in simple dreams, an insistence on small miracles; that we can tuck in our children at night and know that they are fed and clothed and safe from harm; that we can say what we think, write what we think, without hearing a sudden knock on the door; that we can have an idea and start our own business without paying a bribe; that we can participate in the political process without fear of retribution, and that our votes will be counted—at least most of the time.

This year, in this election, we are called to reaffirm our values and our commitments, to hold them against a hard reality and see how we're measuring up to the legacy of our forbearers and the promise of future generations.

And fellow Americans, Democrats, Republicans, Independents, I say to you tonight: We have more work to do—more work to do for the workers I met in Galesburg, Illinois, who are losing their union jobs at the Maytag plant that's moving to Mexico, and now are having to compete with their own children for jobs that pay seven bucks an hour; more to do for the father that I met who was losing his job and choking back the tears, wondering how he would pay $4,500 a month for the drugs his son needs without the health benefits that he counted on; more to do for the young woman in East St. Louis, and thousands more like her, who has the grades, has the drive, has the will, but doesn't have the money to go to college.

Now, don't get me wrong. The people I meet—in small towns and big cities, in diners and office parks—they don't expect government to solve all their problems. They know they have to work hard to get ahead, and they want to. Go into the collar counties around Chicago, and people will tell you they don't want their tax money wasted, by a welfare agency or by the Pentagon. Go in—Go into any inner-city neighborhood, and folks will tell you that government alone can't teach our kids to learn; they know that parents have to teach, that children can't achieve unless we raise their expectations and turn off the television sets and eradicate the slander that says a black youth with a book is acting white. They know those things.

People don't expect—People don't expect government to solve all their problems. But they sense, deep in their bones, that with just a slight change in priorities, we can make sure that every child in America has a decent shot at life, and that the doors of opportunity remain open to all.

They know we can do better. And they want that choice.

In this election, we offer that choice. Our Party has chosen a man to lead us who embodies the best this country has to offer. And that man is John Kerry.

John Kerry understands the ideals of community, faith, and service because they've defined his life. From his heroic service to Vietnam, to his years as a prosecutor and lieutenant governor, through two decades in the United States Senate, he's devoted himself to this country. Again and again, we've seen him make tough choices when easier ones were available.

His values and his record affirm what is best in us. John Kerry believes in an America where hard work is rewarded; so instead of offering tax breaks to companies shipping jobs overseas, he offers them to companies creating jobs here at home.

John Kerry believes in an America where all Americans can afford the same health coverage our politicians in Washington have for themselves.

John Kerry believes in energy independence, so we aren't held hostage to the profits of oil companies, or the sabotage of foreign oil fields.

John Kerry believes in the Constitutional freedoms that have made our country the envy of the world, and he will never sacrifice our basic liberties, nor use faith as a wedge to divide us.

And John Kerry believes that in a dangerous world, war must be an option sometimes, but it should never be the first option.

You know, a while back—a while back I met a young man named Shamus in a VFW Hall in East Moline, Illinois. He was a good-looking kid—six two, six three, clear-eyed, with an easy smile. He told me he'd joined the Marines and was heading to Iraq the following week. And as I listened to him explain why he'd enlisted, the absolute faith he had in our country and its leaders, his devotion to duty and service, I thought this young man was all that any of us might ever hope for in a child.

But then I asked myself, "Are we serving Shamus as well as he is serving us?"

I thought of the 900 men and women—sons and daughters, husbands and wives, friends and neighbors, who won't be returning to their own hometowns. I thought of the families I've met who were struggling to get by without a loved one's full income, or whose loved ones had returned with a limb missing or nerves shattered, but still lacked long-term health benefits because they were Reservists.

When we send our young men and women into harm's way, we have a solemn obligation not to fudge the numbers or shade the truth about why they're going, to care for their families while they're gone, to tend to the soldiers upon their return, and to never ever go to war without enough troops to win the war, secure the peace, and earn the respect of the world.

Now—Now let me be clear. Let me be clear. We have real enemies in the world. These enemies must be found. They must be pursued. And they must be defeated. John Kerry knows this. And just as Lieutenant Kerry did not hesitate to risk his life to protect the men who served with him in Vietnam, President Kerry will not hesitate one moment to use our military might to keep America safe and secure.

John Kerry believes in America. And he knows that it's not enough for just some of us to prosper—for alongside our famous individualism, there's another ingredient in the American saga, a belief that we're all connected as one people. If there is a child on the south side of Chicago who can't read, that matters to me, even if it's not my child. If there is a senior citizen somewhere who can't pay for their prescription drugs, and having to choose between medicine and the rent, that makes my life poorer, even if it's not my grandparent. If there's an Arab-American family being rounded up without benefit of an attorney or due process, that threatens my civil liberties.

It is that fundamental belief—It is that fundamental belief: I am my brother's keeper. I am my sister's keeper that makes this country work. It's what allows us to pursue our individual dreams and yet still come together as one American family.

Now even as we speak, there are those who are preparing to divide us—the spin masters, the negative ad peddlers who embrace the politics of "anything goes." Well, I say to them tonight, there is not a liberal America and a conservative America—there is the United States of America. There is not a Black America and a White America and Latino America and Asian America—there's the United States of America.

The pundits, the pundits like to slice-and-dice our country into Red States and Blue States; Red States for Republicans, Blue States for Democrats. But I've got news for them, too. We worship an "awesome God" in the Blue States, and we don't like federal agents poking around in our libraries in the Red States. We coach Little League in the Blue States and, yes, we've got some gay friends in the Red States. There are patriots who opposed the war in Iraq, and there are patriots who supported the war in Iraq. We are one people, all of us pledging allegiance to the stars and stripes, all of us defending the United States of America.

In the end—In the end—In the end, that's what this election is about. Do we participate in a politics of cynicism, or do we participate in a politics of hope?

John Kerry calls on us to hope. John Edwards calls on us to hope.

I'm not talking about blind optimism here—the almost willful ignorance that thinks unemployment will go away if we just don't think about it, or the health-care crisis will solve itself if we just ignore it.

That's not what I'm talking about. I'm talking about something more substantial. It's the hope of slaves sitting around a fire singing freedom songs; the hope of immigrants setting out for distant shores; the hope of a young naval lieutenant bravely patrolling the Mekong Delta; the hope of a millworker's son who dares to defy the odds; the hope of a skinny kid with a funny name who believes that America has a place for him, too.

Hope—Hope in the face of difficulty. Hope in the face of uncertainty. The audacity of hope!

In the end, that is God's greatest gift to us, the bedrock of this nation. A belief in things not seen. A belief that there are better days ahead.

I believe that we can give our middle class relief and provide working families with a road to opportunity.

I believe we can provide jobs to the jobless, homes to the homeless, and reclaim young people in cities across America from violence and despair.

I believe that we have a righteous wind at our backs and that as we stand on the crossroads of history, we can make the right choices, and meet the challenges that face us.

America! Tonight, if you feel the same energy that I do, if you feel the same urgency that I do, if you feel the same passion that I do, if you feel the same hopefulness that I do—if we do what we must do, then I have no doubt that all across the country, from Florida to Oregon, from Washington to Maine, the people will rise up in November, and John Kerry will be sworn in as President, and John Edwards will be sworn in as Vice President, and this country will reclaim its promise, and out of this long political darkness a brighter day will come.

Thank you very much everybody. God bless you. Thank you.

A great moment in Democratic history: Surrounded by her grandchildren Speaker of the House Nancy Pelosi is sworn in as the first woman speaker at a swearing in ceremony for the 110th Congress, January 4, 2007.

About the Contributors

Brittany Beckman *had her first baby in March 2008, which makes this election year very special for her. She is twenty-one years old, a part-time student, and a lifelong learner.*

Barbara Ann Carle *is a short-story writer, poet, and lifelong Democrat. She is the mother of four and the grandmother of six. One of Barbara's short stories was recently published in* Chicken Soup for the Chocolate Lover's Soul. *She is a retired police officer who resides in Friendswood, Texas, with her husband and family.*

Tracy Douglas *is a law student at Southern Illinois University School of Law. She graduated in May 2006 from the University of Illinois with a journalism degree.*

Stephanie Feuer'*s writing has been published in the* New York Times, *the* New York Daily News, *the* Boston Herald, *the* Real Paper, *and* Sojourner, *and has been performed in* See Me, Hear Me, *a personal essay show in Manhattan. She recently completed a novel set in 1968.*

Darlene Franklin *resides in the Colorado foothills with her mother and her lynx point Siamese cat Talia. She has two grown children and two grandchildren. She loves music, reading, and writing. She has published four books, as well as numerous devotions, magazine articles, and children's curriculum. Visit Darlene's website at www. darlenehfranklin.com.*

D.C. Hall *lives in south Florida. He has retired from the Marines, and has begun a second career as a part-time writer and international sex symbol. (He's serious about the part-time writer thing.) He can be reached at international-symbol@comcast.net.*

Elizabeth Phillips-Hershey'*s article, "An Intergenerational Love Affair," was published in* Chicken Soup for the Coffee Lover's Soul. *She has coauthored a middle-grade children's book,* Mind over Basketball: Coach Yourself to Handle Stress, *and has numerous children's nonfiction stories published in* Appleseeds *and* Faces *by Cobblestone Press. Recent adult publications include* The Aeolian Islands *(2005) and* Sailing the Lycian Coast *(due out in 2008). In 1998, she and her husband, Bob, made a passage across the Atlantic Ocean in their forty-two-foot sailboat. They sailed the Mediterranean Sea for eight years.*

Ramona du Houx *is the editor/writer/publisher of the* Maine Democrat. *The publication reaches 23,000 people throughout the state. She is the author of two children's books,* *the novel* Manitou—A Mythological Journey in Time, *and* Seasons, *a collection of poetry depicting the wonderful inspiration that nature provides throughout the seasons. She is the mother of three grown children, one of whom is currently running for a seat in the Maine House of Representatives. Ramona is also an avid photographer with a website at www.ramonaduhouxphotos.com.*

Georgia A. Hubley *retired after twenty years in financial management to write full-time. She's a frequent contributor to the* Chicken Soup for the Soul *series,* Christian Science Monitor, *and numerous other magazines, newspapers, and anthologies. She resides with her husband of thirty years in Henderson, Nevada. Contact her at GEOHUB@aol.com.*

Lucy James *is the mother of three and a freelance writer who loves to write about her children—which is convenient. She has a regular day job that keeps her busy, but loves burning the midnight oil at the computer, writing as much as she can. She is a liberal Democrat and doesn't mind sharing her views.*

Robyn Kurth *is a freelance writer with more than fifteen years of experience writing and producing corporate and industrial videos, with a specialty in "writing for the ear." A native of the Chicago area, she currently resides in Orlando, Florida, with her husband, Greg, and children, Alex and Zell. One of Ms. Kurth's essays has been published in* Chicken Soup for the Chocolate Lover's Soul. *She can be reached at rwordworks@earthlink.net.*

Audrey Lovell *is a retired dental hygienist who now has the time and luxury to take writing classes and devote herself to creative writing.*

Susan Merson *teaches playwriting at Cal State Fullerton, and has published fiction with Plume and Hugh Lauter Levin, as well as criticism and essays in* Backstage *and* The Loop. *She was a member of the 2007 Bread Loaf Writers Conference and has written the book,* Your Name Here: An Actor/Writer's Guide to Solo Performance. *Visit her website at www.susanmerson.com.*

Linda O'Connell *has published several stories in* Chicken Soup for the Soul *books and other publications.*

Matthue Roth *is a Brooklyn-based reporter and novelist, a performance poet, and a Hasidic Jew. His first novel,* Never Mind the Goldbergs, *was published by Scholastic and is about a teenage Orthodox Jewish girl who accidentally stars on a TV sitcom. His newest book,* Losers, *will be released by Scholastic in September 2008. He has also been published in several anthologies, including the Scholastic collection* This Is PUSH, *Soft Skull Press's* Homewrecker *and* Bottoms Up, *and Dave Eggers's forthcoming anthology,* The Autobiographer's Handbook. *He lives with his wife and daughter in Crown Heights, Brooklyn, and keeps a secret diary at www.matthue.com.*

Matthew J. Rottino *has been an educator for most of his adult life, serving as a teacher, coach, and union leader in New York.*

Nan Schindler Russell *is the author of* Hitting Your Stride: Your Work, Your Way. *She is living her life dream to work and write from the mountains of Montana after a twenty-five-year career in the corporate world. Find out more about Nan at www.nanrussell.com.*

C. A. Verno, *is a South Florida writer specializing in nonfiction short stories, and is a staunch Democrat. He's actively involved in local politics and has worked as a volunteer for every Democratic presidential candidate since Gary Hart, whom he first met while working as a deck hand on the yacht* Monkey Business.

Ferida Wolff *writes essays for newspapers and magazines and has a column on www.seniorwomen.com. She is author of* The Adventures of Swamp Woman: Menopause Essays on the Edge *and seventeen books for children, including the well-reviewed* Is a Worry Worrying You? *written with Harriet May Savitz. Visit her website at www.feridawolff.com.*

Copyright Information

Every Vote Counts. Reprinted by permission of C. A. Verno. © 2008 C. A. Verno.

Howdy Doody Democrat. Reprinted by permission of James Alexander. © 2008 James Alexander.

In Search of the Truth, I Found My Party. Reprinted by permission of Matthew J. Rottino. © 2008 Matthew J. Rottino.

Flashy Campaigning. Reprinted by permission of Scott Gill. © 2008 Scott Gill.

Blue Sheep of the Family. Reprinted by permission of Nancy Ellen Claxton. © 2008 Nancy Ellen Claxton.

Tales of a Mixed Marriage. Reprinted by permission of Barbara Ann Carle. © 2008 Barbara Ann Carle..

Discovery. Reprinted by permission of Ramona du Houx. © 2008 Ramona du Houx

Democrat Versus Republican. Reprinted by permission of Jacqueline Seewald. © 2008 Jacqueline Seewald.

Pressing the Flesh. Reprinted by permission of Susan Merson. © 2008 Susan Merson.

R.E.S.P.E.C.T.. Reprinted by permission of Georgia A. Hubley. © 2008 Georgia A. Hubley.

From Red to Blue: How I Became a Democrat. Reprinted by permission of D. C. Hall. © 2008 D. C. Hall.

A Rising Tide: My Values and Hopes as a Democrat? Reprinted by permission of Brittany Beckman. © 2008 Brittany Beckman.

Getting Along. Reprinted by permission of Ferida Wolff. © 2008 Ferida Wolff.

Children and Politics. Reprinted by permission of Lucy James. © 2008 Lucy James.

Pledge of Allegiance. Reprinted by permission of Stephanie Feuer. © 2008 Stephanie Feuer.

From the Lips of Children. Reprinted by permission of Darlene Franklin. © 2008 Darlene Franklin.

The Only Living Democrat in Brooklyn. Reprinted by permission of Matthue Roth. © 2008 Matthue Roth.

It Takes a Transatlantic Passage. Reprinted by permission of Elizabeth Phillips-Hershey. © 2008 Elizabeth Phillips-Hershey.

The Donkey Club: Memories of a Precinct Captain's Daughter. Reprinted by permission of Myrna Beth Lambert. © 2008 Myrna Beth Lambert.